Getting to know ...
Hidden Lancashire

Ron and Marlene Freethy

PRINTWISE PUBLICATIONS LIMITED

1992

This Edition
© Printwise Publications Ltd 1992

All photographs © Ron Freethy

Published by Printwise Publications Ltd
47 Bradshaw Road, Tottington, Bury, Lancs, BL8 3PW.

Warehouse and Orders
40-42 Willan Industrial Estate, Vere Street,
(off Eccles New Road),
Salford, M5 2GR.
Tel: 061-745 9168 Fax: 061-737 1755

ISBN No. **1 872226 54 X**

Edited by

Cliff Hayes

Printed & bound by Manchester Free Press,
Paragon Mill, Jersey Street,
Manchester M4 6FP.
Tel: 061-236 8822

Introduction & Acknowledgements

We have been walking the highways and byways of Lancashire and the North Country for more than 30 years. We define ourselves more as strollers than walkers as we need time, often lots of time, to explore the history and natural history of the area through which we are passing.

We were pleased when Cliff Hayes suggested that we produce this book of strolls suitable for those who enjoy a meal in a hotel or taking a picnic. We were invited to update some walks which we published in the early 1980s and which have now changed for the better. The present book is dedicated to those who are frightened by maps and long strenuous walks but who love being out in the open air in beautiful countryside.

We are grateful to friends who suggested new walks which are included here or who allowed us to use their photographs when our own library proved lacking. To Carole Pugh we are grateful for the exquisite drawings.

Our thanks are also due to the Editor of the Lancashire Evening Telegraph who, over the last 23 years has published Freethy's Countryscene, a weekly feature and which has ensured that we have to do at least one walk each week. Some of this material is included in the present volume.

Finally we thank one energetic black labrador who insists that we walk throughout the year and in all weathers — a sure way to discover the secrets of an area.

Ron Freethy

About the Authors

Ron Freethy is President of the North East Lancashire Rambler's Association and has made many television and radio programmes. With his wife Marlene he has written several walking books and volumes on tourism throughout the country. The couple live in the Pendle area and are thus an ideal choice to prepare this book and the companion volumes.

Marlene Freethy with Bono ... always an excuse for a walk

Dunsop Bridge is a favourite spot with paddlers, picknickers and gentle strollers.

Contents

Around Bleasdale

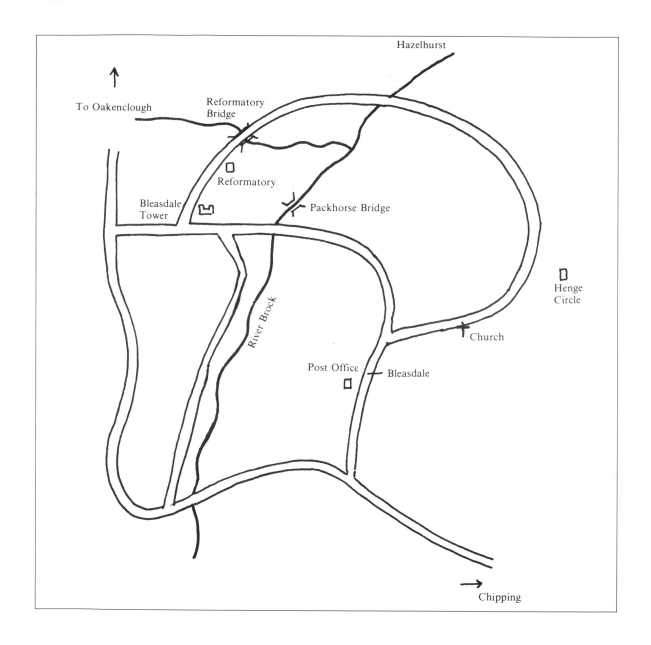

Walk One
Around Bleasdale

ACCESS:

From Clitheroe follow the signs towards Longridge. Follow the signs to Chipping and then towards Oakenclough. Bleasdale is signed to the right. The Post Office has a pleasant little cafe and an area selling books and maps.

ROUTE:

From the car the road is followed towards Garstang until an obvious track leads off to the right. Follow this over a delightful bridge and past the Old Reformatory on the right. Continue over another bridge to the old settlement of Hazelhurst. Retrace your steps to the Post Office but take your time because this is delightful country. Also from the Post Office there is an obvious road leading past the school to the parish church of St. Eadmer.

OUR WALK:

Set into a hollow between the ancient markets of Garstang and Chipping, Bleasdale is a charming but tiny settlement surrounded by lovely fields and interesting buildings. We parked the car opposite the post office which doubles as a small cafe and bookshop. The building itself is a converted blacksmith's forge which must have been busy when the packhorse trains passed through. Looking at the building today it takes very little imagination to conjure up thoughts of a glowing forge, the sound of hot iron being struck, sparks flying, horses snorting and the smith eager for news and quizzing the packhorse driver.

On the day of our visit there was a hint of rain in the

Bleasdale Post Office, an ideal base for two pleasant strolls.

heavy air and swallows, swifts and house martins hawked low over the water of the Higher Brock stream overhung with sweet smelling hawthorn blossom, alder and gorse and beneath these was a colourful tangle of summer flowers including bluebell, red campion and the white star-like blossoms of stitchwort.

A circular walk of around four miles leads from the post office, passes Bleasdale school and the church before sweeping across to a group of farms and an old reformatory before returning to the post office. This is longer and a little more strenuous than most in this book for strollers. Most visitors may, therefore, prefer to take two separate and more gentle strolls with a break for lunch and this is the pattern which we followed.

Beyond the school and fringed by meadows gleaming with golden buttercups we soon reached the parish church of St.

Eadmer of Admarsh in Bleasdale, a pale coloured building looking much older than it really is. It was actually constructed in 1835 by John Dewhurst with an extensive addition being made to the chancel in 1897. It is the two west windows, however, which give the feeling of antiquity and it is thought that these came from an Elizabethan church which the new structure replaced. An enquiry into the condition of the church in 1650 reported that it was in a sad state of repair. St Eadmer was a religious writer of the 12th century so it may well be that a third church of even earlier vintage existed on the site.

An even more ancient religion was practiced in the private fields beyond Vicarage Farm. Here was sited a Wood Henge, now indicated by concrete filled holes whilst the few remnants have been removed to the Harris Museum in Preston

Bleasdale Parish Church reached by a pleasant road lined by rich hedgerow.

for safe keeping. We often think that we do not take enough interest in the prehistoric sites in our part of England. There is no doubt that the Bleasdale Circle is an important site in a lovely setting below the slopes of Fairsnape Fell. When illuminated by morning sunlight or in frost, scrapes known as 'sledge rows' are easily visible. These mark the route taken by loads of peat shunted down from the moorland to fire the hearths of Bleasdale and perhaps even the old smithy itself.

After lunch we strolled a short distance along the road towards Garstang before turning to the right along a beautiful leafy lane which eventually descended to a bridge over the evocatively named Baby Brock river. Beyond this 'new bridge' is a magnificent packhorse bridge set in a fairylike dell, with ferns dripping from its span and the sweet smell of honeysuckle filling the air in late summer. The road continues to the so called Reformatory, built in 1857 by William James Garnett (1818-1873) who lived at Bleasdale Tower. Garnett set out to provide city boys who had been in trouble with a little discipline and a lot of much needed skills including farming and shoemaking. The building is in a most delightful setting and provided some 30 boys with an environment which must have been better than anything they had been accustomed to in the slums of the city. A short distance past the Reformatory is yet another bridge and this was built by the lads themselves and it stands so strong today that it is a fitting tribute to the workers and, of course, their teachers. On one side is a plaque recording the boys' efforts and on the other is a series of carvings depicting the various tools used in the construction. The Reformatory building has now been converted into houses for the estate workers (the land is now owned by the Duckworth family) who still talk of Mr Bullock the clogger who first came to Bleasdale as a city lad "in need of correction." A salutary tale is also told of 'difficult' characters being roped to a plough and used like horses to get

The Old Reformatory has now been converted into dwelling houses.

rid of their excess energy!

The walk continues to a farm known as Hazelhurst which is the one remaining habitation in what was once a substantial settlement. During the 16th century almost 20 families lived under the shelter of Hazelhurst fell and judging by the presence of the stone supports of the stocks not all were law abiding. There is always a sad feeling when standing in the centre of a deserted village and this is no exception. Huddled close to an ancient but healthy looking elm tree are a number of old buildings in varying stages of decay. We closed our eyes and conjured up the sound of pigs, hens, cattle lowing, the laughter and perhaps crying of children. We opened our eyes and looked at the 'sledge roads' up on Hazelhurst fells and marvelled at the toughness of folk who achieved self-sufficiency in these potentially inhospitable if scenically beautiful surroundings. The rain which had threatened all day now began to fall and somehow it seemed right to leave Hazelhurst in its own misty little hollow.

As we turned our backs on the past and began the return journey to Bleasdale Post Office the sun managed to break through and reflected from the plumage of an albino pheasant which was feeding, along with many others being reared on the well keepered estate. A dipper fed its young under the old packhorse bridge. It is surprising how local folk take their own countryside for granted. We are used to the perky white bibbed dipper along our streams but on this walk we were accompanied by a friend from the lowland south of England. Her excitement was intense as she watched the first dipper of her life! As we moved off rather suddenly we scared a woodpigeon which soon recovered and soared upwards and then produced a sharp cracking noise with its wings. This is the way the male displays to his mate.

This particular area is one which proves that you do not have to scramble up steep paths or cover vast distances to strike into beautiful and lonely countryside.

Hawthorn blossom is a feature of Bowland in spring.

Honeysuckle adds
a delightful smell
to the hedgerows.

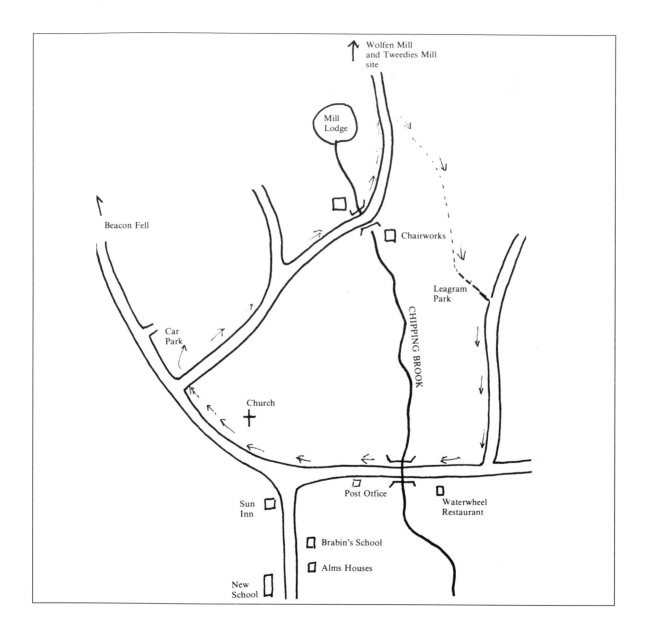

16

Walk Two
Around Chipping

ACCESS:

Leave Clitheroe on the B6243. Follow the Longridge road to a cross road at the Halls Inn at Knowle Green. Turn right and follow the road up to another cross roads dominated by the New Drop Inn. Chipping is signed straight ahead and in the village there is a large car park with good toilets. There are excellent cafes and hotels in the village and both the New Drop and the Halls Inn are good places to eat.

THE ROUTE:

From the car park turn left in front of the church and follow the road to a junction. Bear right and descend to Berry's chair works. Climb steep road and pass the old mill lodge on the left. Opposite the pond find a footpath indicated right. This leads through the grounds of Leagram Park. As the track meets the road turn right and then right again passing the Waterwheel Restaurant. Proceed through the village allowing time for exploring and thence back to the car park. There are plenty of good pubs in the village and also coffee shops. Chipping caters very well for tourists and the ice cream on sale here is worth travelling miles to sample.

OUR WALK:

Anyone driving or walking around Bowland can be excused for thinking that all roads lead to Chipping. This ancient village was once one of the most important markets and it was therefore vital to mark the route to Chipping from every point of the

17

John Brabbin's School and Almshouses at Chipping.

compass. Whilst the 'bus service is not the most regular there is a large car park in the village and well signed walks indicate gentle strolls into the heart of the Vale of Chipping. One of our favourites has the advantage of being circular and begins from the car park near the church and heads initially towards Parlick Pike. The energetic can follow the well trodden route to the top and listen to the hill top birds including lapwing, curlew and golden plover. The human species has always envied birds the power of flight and an increasing number of intrepid hang gliders now hurl themselves from the slopes of Parlick and soar over the colourful meadows and patchwork patterns of the hamlets clustered around Chipping.

Our favourite form of exercise is far more sedate and our route descends towards Berry's chairworks, a thriving concern utilising an old cotton mill situated opposite a group of

A grand old Bentley outside one of Chipping's old pubs.

fascinating old cottages and near to the one time village workhouse. We chose a splendid day and the hot sun was beating down from a clear blue sky as we crossed the bridge over Chipping Brook. At the side of the bridge is a flight of well worn steps which would have been essential to reach the stream in the days prior to piped water. All washing was done in the stream on the banks of which we found several healthy looking clumps of horsetails which are primitive plants related to the ferns and which once grew to heights of 50 feet (15.2 metres) when the climate of Britain was more tropical than it is today. In the Carboniferous period some 345 million years ago these swamp-loving plants were prolific, grew quickly but had a short life span. The weight of freshly dead plants crushed those beneath and eventually produced the 'fossil fuel' which we call coal. The climate is now too harsh and only a few of the smaller horsetails have managed to survive but in the not too distant past they were invaluable to the housewife. They contain

a great deal of sand (silica) in their tissues and are therefore almost as rough as sandpaper. They were formerly used as pan and pot scrubbers.

Despite the sometimes feverish and always fascinating activity at the chairworks it is always worthwhile sitting in the vicinity with your eyes closed. Sounds of huge trees being sawn into workable planks, the whine of sanding machinery smoothing the wood and the clanking of the chains on the machinery never succeeds in swamping the calls of the birds in the nearby living trees whilst the smell of sawdust and acetone-based varnishes it almost – but not quite – overcome the scent of new cut grass. Although Berry's is a go-ahead modern industry known world wide for the traditional design of their chairs the atmosphere of a rural, almost woodland based, industry remains inescapable.

At one time there were five water mills powered by Chipping Brook and apart from the chairworks another has been converted into a fine and popular restaurant sensibly called the Waterwheel. Wolfen Mill which once made bobbins and then functioned as a cheese factory was in a derelict condition and looked ready for demolition by the 1950s. It has now been tastefully converted into a residence of great charm and character. A footpath leads up to the old mill lodge which is popular with a variety of wildfowl. Whilst we were admiring the building a weasel eased its way, low slung and snake-like, out of a wall. It looked cheekily around to see what was going on and then twisted its way across the narrow road and vanished into a patch of nettles. These swayed when they were touched, disturbing a female small tortoiseshell butterfly which had been laying her eggs on the leaves.

Between the mill lodge of Berry's chairworks and Wolfen Mill was Chipping Brook's more unusual mill, which has sadly been demolished. Tweedies began life as a cotton mill, but eventually earned a world wide reputation in maritime circles.

How strange to find water turbines, portholes and other ship fitments being produced by craftsmen based so far inland. Orders were received during the construction of Thomas Lupton's fine ship 'The Shamrock' and Tweedies mill was very busy up to the mid 1950s when shipbuilding began its sad decline. It is reasonable to suppose that the inland "support factories" would be the first to suffer as everyone struggled to cut costs in order to remain competitive in a shrinking maritime market. All traces of the mill have now gone.

The winding road with its flower-strewn hedgerows twists and turns its way back into Chipping with its lovely old houses dominated by Saint Bartholomew's, one of the district's most beautiful churches. Chipping's own brook is actually a tributary of the river Loud and the valley must have been subject to regular flooding before effective drainage techniques evolved. The valley bottom must have been far too wet and unhealthy to support any permanent settlement. Malaria was a common disease of medieval Britain and the lowland swamps were a breeding ground for the blood sucking mosquitoes which transmitted the disease from one person to another. For this reason the rocky knoll on which the church stands was ideal not only for St. Bartholmew's but also for the market. This combination of trade and religion was not unusual during this period. Look in the churchyard for the sundial dated 1708 but study the base carefully. This is probably part of the old market cross.

A church stood on this spot from at least AD1041 but the main part of the present building dates from 1240 and there were extensive additions and rebuilding in both the 15th and 16th centuries whilst the sturdy tower is dated at 1450. Extensive restoration was undertaken in 1873 but the overall appearance of the building would seem not to have been significantly altered. There are Holy Water stoupes scattered

throughout the interior of the church and a Piscina which was part of original 12th century church. The font has been dated to 1520 and is thought to have been given by the Bradley family whose initials are carved on one of several shields around the font. Other carvings show details of Christ's Passion. Easily distinguishable are nails, scourges, hammer and pincers. Two blank shields are something of a mystery, but there are signs that the original carvings were removed. This may have been the doings of a zealous Puritan and some historians have

The old abattoir at Chipping.

suggested that the carvings are of the Five Wounds of Christ or perhaps the Holy Heart. The "Saxon Runes" which are carved around the base might not have survived if the Puritans had stocd on their heads and discovered that these were not runes but inverted initials which read A M G P D T. This is thought to relate to a section from the gospel of St Luke chapter one verse 28. Ave Maria Gratia Plena Dominus Tocum which translates as Hail Mary thou that art highly favoured, the Lord is with thee.

The Shireburn family were influential in Bowland for many centuries but are usually remembered for their magnificent house at Stoneyhurst and the family tombs in Great Mitton church. Chipping was also influenced by the family and there was once a Shireburn chantry here which was also known as the Wolfhouse Quire referring to the family home at Wolfen Hall. A chantry had far too many Roman Catholic overtones for the

Puritans and many were ripped out with a complete disregard for damage done to the fabric of the building. All that remains of the old chantry is a Holy Water stoupe, but it was sited close to the Berry Memorial window. This lovely piece of modern stained glass commemorates the life of the founder of the chairworks. The original function of stained glass in churches was to tell a story in pictures to those who were unable to read. They were thus the original visual aid used by priests who were also the medieval teaching profession. It is always good to see the tradition maintained and looking at the Berry window it is easy to study the art of chair making. Another of the Church's functions was to assist in healing the sick either using faith or medicine. It is interesting to read the list of Chipping's rectors beginning with Robert in AD 1230 who was followed ten years later by Peter the Physician.

If the visitor descends the steps from the churchyard and turns left the real beauty of the village is soon appreciated. We must pause by the gates, however, and relate an interesting story which unfolds when a wedding party is leaving after the ceremony. Known as "Perrying" the local children secure the gate with rope and refuse to open it until coins are thrown down the steps and which are scrambled for with a surprisingly fierce determination.

The first village building reached is the old butcher's shop now closed and replaced by a modern complex at the top of the village. By the side of the old shop is a narrow alleyway down which the animals were driven and were unable to turn before entering the slaughter house. In Old English the word "Chipping" meant market and the butcher's shop with its attached abattoir is just one example of how self contained it must have been. Walk down the narrow, well named Windy Street where there always seems to be a breeze, to Brabins (or Brabyns) school built with money given by a Quaker benefactor who died in 1683. John

Brabin made his fortune as a dyer and cloth dealer. On Talbot Street, the main thoroughfare of the village, is the post office and craft shop. A plaque on the wall informs us that here was Brabin's shop, office and home. The old school is now used as a youth club and a new building still carrying his name is attended by the local children receiving their primary education. It is rather nice to think of the blue coated Brabin scholars trudging down the cobbled street to meet their master who lived in an adjacent house also provided by the founder. High standards were set and in his will Brabin ordered that any master falling short was to be instantly "put out" by the governors.

Even for those who do not follow our route, no visit to Chipping would be complete without a gentle stroll past the Waterwheel Restaurant and turning left towards Leagram. If the bridlepath signed to Stanley is followed for a short distance it takes us backwards in time into the grounds of Leagram Hall surely some of the most magnificent rolling parkland to be found anywhere in Britain. Leagram began as a medieval deer park, but many of the splendid trees including ash and oak would probably have been known to the owner John Weld who was a fine naturalist and who kept detailed diaries of his observations between 1850 and 1886. In September 1856 he reported a swallow which was "dull white without a single coloured feather about it, the eye was black with a beautiful bright yellow rim encircling it."

During our stroll through the park we sought shelter from the broiling sun beneath a spreading ash and looked in vain for a white swallow among the large number swooping low over the fields full of cattle. The birds were obviously catching the flies which were attracted to the cow pats. Far too soon it was time to return to Chipping which never fails to delight the naturalist and historian alike. It handles its visitors well and never loses the air of old world serenity.

A skilled chair worker hard at work at Berry's factory based in an old cotton mill at Chipping.

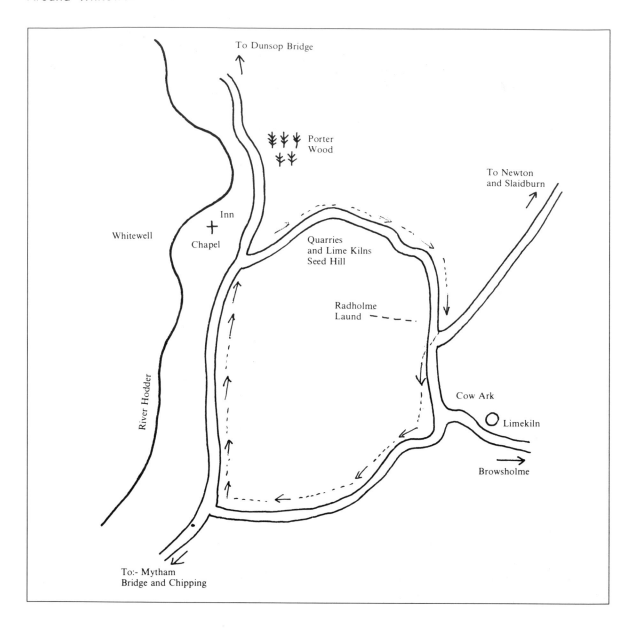

To Dunsop Bridge

Porter
Wood

To Newton
and Slaidburn

Inn

Whitewell

Chapel

Quarries
and Lime Kilns
Seed Hill

Radholme
Laund

River Hodder

Cow Ark

Limekiln

Browsholme

To:- Mytham
Bridge and Chipping

Walk Three
Around Whitewell

ACCESS:

From Whalley take the road to Great Mitton, pass over the Ribble bridge and pass the Three Fishes Hotel on the left. At a cross roads continue straight ahead, signed Trough of Bowland. Continue to follow the Trough of Bowland signs as the road passes through Whitewell. There is limited parking in the village in the region of the Whitewell Inn.

THE ROUTE:

From the Whitewell Inn follow the top road to Cow Ark via Seed Hill. The road climbs very steeply but there are seats strategically placed. Pass disused lime kilns on the right and then onwards passing Radholme Laund. From Cow Ark follow the road back to Whitewell. Although much of this walk is along roads they are so narrow and close to glorious scenery that this does not matter.

OUR WALK:

When is a forest not a forest? We think of a huge expanse of trees with a tangle of undergrowth, but to our Saxon ancestors the forest was a place to hunt wild beasts including wolves, wildcat, wild boar, pine martens and of course deer. When the invading Normans took over the forests there were obviously plenty of trees but there were also large open areas across which they could hunt. Two of the best gallops were within the forests of Rossendale and Bowland. Although many of Bowland's trees have now been felled, there has been a lot of replanting in recent

The Blackcap is a summer visiting warbler which breeds in the woodlands among the undergrowth.

years although conifers have predominated. The walk from Whitewell to Cow Ark enables us to understand how the old forest was managed.

Whitewell was the old administrative centre of the forest, the chief officer being a master forester and his deputy was known as the bow bearer. Before the building of the inn at Whitewell, a lodge existed and functioned as a combination between an office and a courtroom.Peasants could be punished for the offences of venison (killing deer) and vert (cutting down timber). They were only allowed to take small branches for their fires and only those rotting branches which they could reach using a hook or a crook. Here we have the origin of the phrase "By hook or by crook", when we speak of doing something despite opposition.

Whitewell's chapel began in 1422 as a chapel of ease in which a corpse could be deposited for the night on its way for burial in a properly consecrated church. Whitewell church is now administered from Chipping. In 1836, the church of St Michael was rebuilt and is now overlooked by a lime tree which produces so much nectar that it seems to be full of drunken bees during the summer and early autumn. Inside the church is a fine Flemish tapestry on loan from Browsholme Hall. The Whitewell Inn provides a welcome for the walkers and for fishermen who find good sport in the River Hodder which bends around Whitewell. This is one of the finest salmon and trout stretches in the north west.

The stroll to Cow Ark begins with a stiff climb up Hall Hill and in the heat of a summer's day we were more than glad to make use of a seat provided in memory of John and Mary Edwards. This had been sensibly sited at the summit overlooking a quarry and a disused lime kiln was being used by a pair of pied wagtails and a pair of pigeons to raise their hungry families whose cries echoed around the arches of the building.

The quarry, long disused contains many fascinating fossils including sea lilies, showing that this part of Bowland was once submerged beneath a shallow sea. As Bowland changed gradually from a forest to an agriculture society, the quarry must have been vital for building material and for the lime to neutralise the natural acidity of the soil.

A look at the map, however, will take us back to the forest. A farm known as Radholme Laund refers to its origins as a deer enclosure, while just beyond is another farm called Park Gate which was obviously just that. Both native red and the lovely spotted Fallow deer probably introduced by the Normans were emparked here.

From the early 15th century, deer became less and less important, and the Parkers of Browsholme were switching their allegiance from deer to cattle.

Cow Ark is now a pretty but insignificant settlement, reflecting this change in land use. Opposite the telephone box is a finger post informing us that we are six miles from Clitheroe, $19\frac{1}{2}$ from Lancaster and three miles from Whitewell, unless we wish to return along our route via Hall Hill which is only one and a half miles.

On the day of our walk, rain during the night had been followed by a hot morning and in conditions like this the scents of plants carry over a wide area. The ramsons near the river bottom under the bridge at Cow Ark fill the valley with the strong smell of garlic. Further along the road back to Hall Hill a strong smell of aniseed enabled us to find a relative of the carrot family which is called sweet cecily. Meadow sweet, a member of the rose family added its sweetness and we also found water mint in a damp hedge. Colour, if not aroma, was added by the deep blue of germander speedwell and the shining yellow of silverweed. One discovery, however, took us straight back to

Both the wildcat (this page) and the wolf (opposite) were once common in the Forest of Bowland. Both were hunted to extinction many centuries ago.

the old forest of Bowland. This was a patch of dog's mercury. This plant spreads very slowly and only grows in woods. What was it doing miles away from woodlands? It is what botanists call an indicator species and tells us that the area was once covered in trees. We know it was but it is nice to have it proved.

There are many other little strolls around Whitewell which is one of the finest Inns in the county and set on a fold in the River Hodder. After a substantial bar snack some strollers prefer to wander up and down the riverside footpaths. Here is one of the best salmon rivers in Britain and a birdwatcher's paradise.

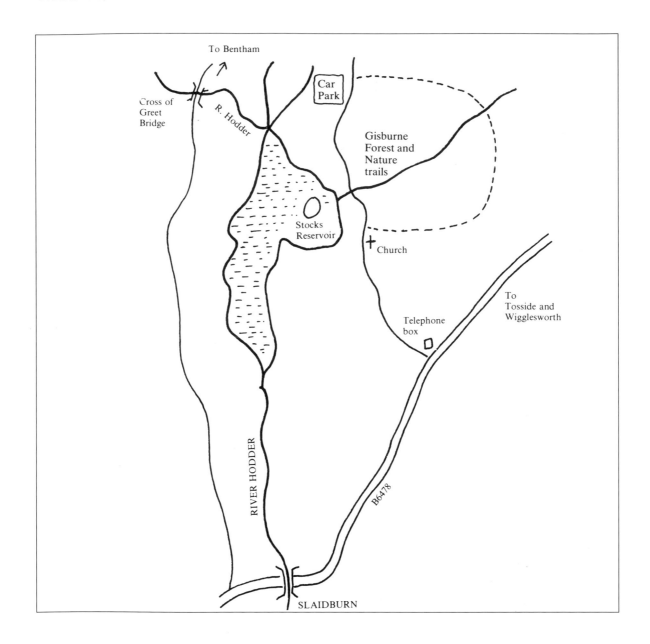

Walk Four
Stocks Reservoir

ACCESS:

From Slaidburn follow main road out of the village over the bridge spanning the Hodder. The road winds and climbs steeply passing a number of farms. At a cross roads where there is a telephone box turn left. This leads past a number of car parks and picnic sites before descending towards the reservoir and passing a small church on the right. Continue to a substantial car park on the left hand side close to a bend in the road. There are no toilets at this point but there are adequate facilities at Slaidburn where there are also cafes and a pub.

THE ROUTE:

We have chosen one of the shorter routes from the picnic site close to the reservoir. The views are excellent and the route passes close to one of the most interesting churches in the county. From the car park follow the narrow road up to the right. Then follow the nature trail through and around the forest. Descend towards the road and enjoy lovely views of the reservoir. Turn right through a tree lined path to the road. Cross the road and turn right; then follow the path back to the car park.

OUR WALK:

The infant waters of the River Hodder once flowed along a pebbled bed through the village of Stocks, which should perhaps be more accurately referred to as Dale Head. We descended from the highlands above Tosside and felt the full force of the north easterly wind which whipped ice into our faces and each sharp

The Whitewell Inn overlooking the River Hodder is a fine place to eat, stay or fish having one of the finest angling stretches in Britain at its rear.

piece brought its own sharp sting. There did seem the chance of a clear spell of weather and we were glad to find temporary sanctuary from the elements in St. James Church at Dalehead. We took off our gloves and blew hard on our hands to restore some circulation. What a contrast this was from our previous visit on a steamy hot and sticky day when the churchyard smelled of freshly cut grass and the borders were strewn with wild flowers including both marsh and common spotted orchids, red common sorrel, bright yellow tormentil and the more delicate shades of lady's mantle. But January weather in these high places is altogether different and we found ourselves eagerly longing for the warmth of a cottage or an inn's log fire blazing in the hearth. Alas Dalehead can no longer provide such a luxury as a glance at a rather forlorn notice on the wall of the church bears witness. It tells us that not far from the present church the old village lies submerged beneath the waters of the Fylde Water Board's Stock's reservoir. There were once some twenty houses, a shop, post office and a pub called 'The New Inn'. Stand on the Clapham road and look out over the water towards the

The Whitewell Chapel, once a chapel-of-ease set deep in the forest.

grassy island which in summer echoes to the strident calls of breeding black headed gulls. The village lay just to the right of the island and in times of severe drought the foundations of the old buildings can be seen. A few foundations can be seen on the edge of the 'lake'. The Fylde Water Board Act of 1925 sealed the fate of the village and the demolition of the buildings began. On November 12th 1926 the Bishop of Bradford consecrated a new burial ground above the water level and on 30th July 1938 the present church was consecrated having been built with stone from the original church. This was not very old and only consecrated in 1852. Evensong is held every third Sunday which always reminds us of a mellow October evening when we had been bird watching and the sound of Canada geese returning to their roost mingled with the gentle refrain of a hymn. We closed our eyes and gave a silent prayer for the old folk of Dalehead and wondered how many tears they shed as they watched the waters rising against the new dam and swamping their homes, church and pub. Think how you would feel if forced to watch your home drowned!

If the villagers returned they would not recognise very much of the surrounding scenery. The Forestry Commission have also been active and have clothed the hillsides with conifers although some native trees and shrubs remain including birch, alder, hazel and dog rose. At one time the Commission were most reluctant to allow visitors into their plantations but in recent years this attitude has mellowed. Parking spaces are provided and well designed nature walks penetrate the forest and climb to some delightfully scenic picnic spots. The trails have even been graded. The red trail takes an estimated 75 minutes in contrast to the strolls of 50 minutes along the white route and a gentle 40 minutes following the blue arrows. At Hollins Bay a day permit for fishing may be obtained, but it is the naturalist, especially the winter bird watcher, who has most to gain from a visit to Stocks. The strength of the site is its variety of habitat. From the trails panoramic views over the 344 acre (137 hectares) reservoir can reveal winter flocks of Canada geese, tufted duck,

The Japanese larch is one of the commonest trees around Stocks Reservoir.

WIGEON

TEAL

MALLARD

GOOSANDER

TUFTED DUCK

Stocks Reservoir has many species of wildfowl, each of which feeds at a different level as shown in this drawing by Carole Pugh.

pochard, mallard, teal, wigeon and goldeneye. Birds of prey include sparrowhawk, kestrel, tawny and long eared owl plus rarities such as osprey, goshawk and hen harrier. The reservoir is surrounded by the 4000 acres of Gisburn Forest which although quite dense can often reward careful watchers with sightings of woodcock, jay, raven, redstart, barn owl with flocks of crossbills occasionally passing through in autumn. Above the trees on the rolling moorland short eared owl and both black and red grouse are seen along with the more common species such as skylark, meadow pipit and wheatear.

The area has been made much more accessible since the new car parks and paths have been opened and most of the walks are very gentle whilst the serious walker can find more strenuous exercise by following one of several tracks over the Bowland Fells.

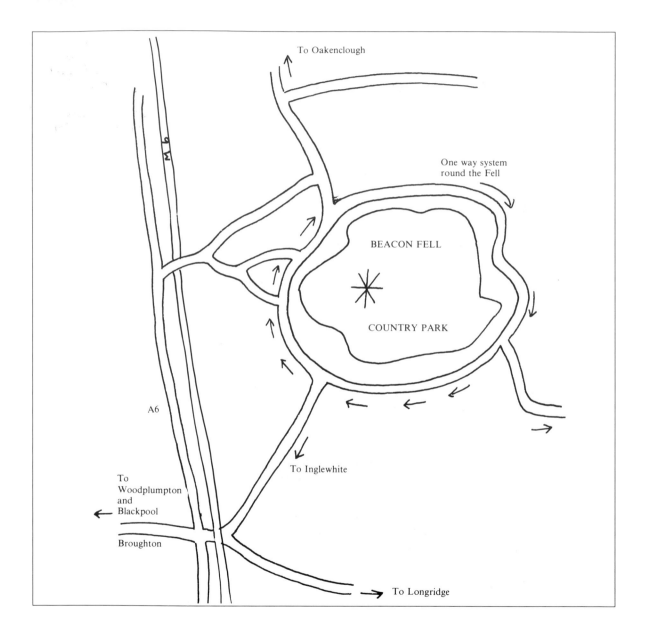

Walk Five
Beacon Fell

ACCESS:

Beacon is about 8 miles to the north of Preston and signposted off the A6 at Broughton. It is also well signed from Longridge.

THE ROUTE:

This is a wonderful place to picnic and the path is well marked and easy to follow. Having chosen your initial direction the path simply skirts around the hill passing in and out of conifer plantations through clearings from which there are lovely views.

OUR WALK:

Although Beacon Fell is only 873 feet (266 metres) its mainly conifer clad summit dominates the plain of West Lancashire with Blackpool clearly visible on a good day whilst to the east Bowland is laid out in all its splendour. No wonder it has been used as one of a chain of beacon hills since the Bronze Age. By lighting fires on the summits vital signals could be transmitted with surprising speed. Those of us who walk the hills, however, know only too well that we can suffer for days on end under heavy rain and low swirling clouds. Invading forces would quickly have learned to attack during periods of poor visibility.

Beacon Fell has now been designated as a Country Park and spread among its 185 acres are numerous car parks and a visitors centre is usually open at weekends although unfortunately not during the week. Very sensibly a one way system for cars has been marked along the narrow road which spirals its way to the summit. Whilst the majority of trees around the fell are

41

commercially grown conifers there are many native species including oak, ash, rowan and silver birch. Among the conifers are spruce, pine and larch. There is a simple way of distinguishing between the three. All you have to do is to try to pull off a leaf. Spruce leaves come off singly, pine leaves break off in pairs whilst the larch leaves come away in lumps. Thus we have S for spruce and single, P for pine and pair and L for both larch and lump! This is a rough and ready rule but it works most of the time. Two sorts of spruce are grown commercially and are sold as Christmas trees. Norway spruce is the European species although it never occurs naturally in Britain. Its foliage is soft and both the upper and lower surfaces of the leaves are bright green. These are ideal for Christmas trees whilst the foliage of the sitka spruce from North America (Sitka is a town in Canada) is green on top, grey green beneath and is very prickly. Next time you buy your tree ask for Norway spruce and you will find it much more comfortable to decorate!

This mixture of trees encourage a rich and varied wildlife to Beacon fell. The majority of visitors, however, arrive in the

Jays are common breeders in the conifers around Beacon Fell

middle of the day when the birds and beasts are having a quiet siesta but those who can arrive early and leave late will have much more to observe. We arrived just as the sun was rising and the pink flush of dawn was providing a soft blush over Bowland. Without getting out of the car we wound down the window and had a quiet cup of coffee and a cold bacon sandwich. Out of the undergrowth came a long tailed field mouse which ran along a dead moss covered branch. Also known as the woodmouse this attractive creature can climb trees every bit as well as a squirrel and also uses its long tail as an organ of balance. A grunting snuffling noise indicated that a hedgehog was taking a late breakfast before seeking out a comfortable spot in which to sleep out the day.

Even though it was late June the sound of the birds coming to life was dramatic, and among the choir we recognised song thrush, blackbird, robin, wren, blackcap and willow warbler. A cock pheasant called loudly and cattle and sheep joined in from the fields below to welcome the new day. A treecreeper worked its way spirally up an old birch covered with bracket fungus.

Wildroses are a feature of the hedgerows during June and July

This used to be called the razor strop fungus because it was so tough and rubbery that it was used to sharpen the old cut throat razors and also the bill hooks which were used when laying hedges and cutting through vegetation. Sunlight was slinking through a patch of nettles and red admiral was spreading wide its wings to catch every ray of heat. Butterflies are cold blooded and the cooler they are the slower they move and are therefore more vulnerable to predators. They therefore spend the early morning soaking up the sun which is their equivalent to a Grand Prix driver revving up prior to the start of the race.

Beacon Fell also has its share of interesting plants including blackberries and cranberries which attract late summer and autumn visitors fired with a desire to live off the land. Around the fell are a number of small ponds in which grow yellow flag and arrowhead the latter so named because of the shape of its leaves. Gerard, the 16th century herbalist called it the water archer, but did not recommend it as a cure for any illness. This is not surprising because it was a plant recommended by those who practiced the Doctrines of Signatures. This suggests that God had put His sign on each and every plant to tell us what they could be used for. Those wounded by an arrow were therefore ritualistically dosed with a brew made by dropping nine dried leaves of arrowhead into hot water. The fact that Gerard, who was very skilled for the age in which he lived, did not include it in his herbal suggests that it was useless.

Beacon Fell has many virtues and the good parking and well marked paths so rich in wildlife all combine to ensure a regular flow of visitors. Despite this the cover given by the trees can give the feeling of being alone despite the close proximity of other visitors.

The woodmouse, also known as the long tailed field mouse is common around Beacon Fell

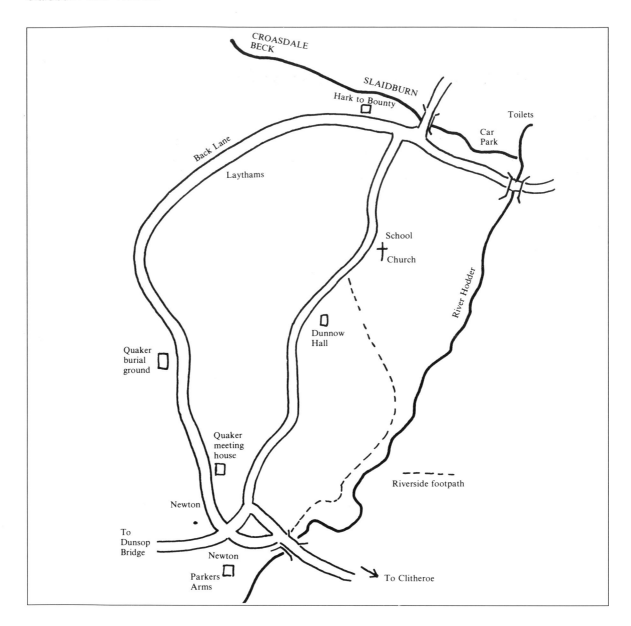

Walk Six
Slaidburn and Newton

ACCESS:
Take the B6478 out of Clitheroe and follow the back road towards Long Preston passing through West Bradford and Newton. There is ample parking in the village, especially close to the bridge over the River Hodder.

THE ROUTE:
From the village follow the road and pass the church on the left. Look out for a footpath signed to the left. This follows the line of the Hodder and up to the right is Dunnow Hall. Pass through an area of light woodland and continue to Newton Bridge. Turn right over the bridge and continue to the Parker Arms. Turn left and then right up Back Lane passing the Quaker Meeting House on the right. Continue along the road and return to Slaidburn alongside Croasdale Beck.

OUR WALK:
There can be no better walk than the one connecting these two beautiful and historic villages. This gentle stroll has the added bonus of following the meanderings of the Hodder, one of the prettiest and least polluted of any river in Britain. There is only one fault – a single day is hardly sufficient to appreciate what is on offer.

Slaidburn has two fine bridges one spanning the Hodder and the other its tributary Croasdale Beck, which is almost as substantial as the main stream itself. A lovely gently rising footpath follows Croasdale Beck through pretty woodland and a

47

Slaidburn's church is one of the finest in the area.

former corn mill can be seen from Jubilee gardens with the mill leat and pond both clearly visible. Rabbit breeding was once one of the village industries the pelts being used for making hats. The main car park is below the village and alongside the Hodder with its graceful bridge carrying traffic towards Stocks-in-Bowland and Tosside. A stroll up into the village leads past a tea shop and a fine war memorial to one of Bowland's most famous inns. Hark to Bounty until 1861 was known as the Dog Inn but it is then alleged that whilst the Master of the Hunt was taking refreshment he heard his favourite dog eager to continue the sport and he said "Just Hark to Bounty" and the name stuck. When the old court house was demolished local justice was meted out in a room above the bar at the Hark to Bounty. A window at the rear of the pub which is studded with coloured glass is probably a remnant of the old court the site of which is still remembered in the name of a field – Court House Close. There was once a second pub in the village and named the Black Bull but this is now used as a Youth Hostel. It is on the corner almost opposite Hark to Bounty. The start of the gentle stroll to the village of Newton begins at the church of St. Andrew, parts of which were constructed as early as the 12th century but it is on the site of an even earlier settlement. The name Slaidburn probably means a sheep field overlooking a river. This description is still true today and a look into the fields adjacent to the church will also reveal a number of cultivation terraces called lynchets which were typical of Anglo-Saxon agriculture. The tower of the church is a mighty structure which seems to have provided protection during the Scots' raids of 1322 when their confidence was sky high after Bruce's victory at Bannockburn. Outside in the churchyard is a sundial the base of which might well be part of the old market cross. Once more we see Church and commerce

Slaidburn Grammar School is still in use, but now the base for Juniors.

49

The brown hare can be seen in many of the fields between Slaidburn and Newton.

working together. A third facet is also evident in Slaidburn – education. The old Grammar school has a date stone of 15 May 1717 which records the generosity of a farmer named John Brennand who funded the extensions. Attached to this historic building are the modern buildings of the village junior school. There are two road routes from Slaidburn to Newton but the footpath along the river is one of the finest strolls in Bowland.

On this stroll we have a favourite tree – a gnarled old alder. Late in April we watched a kingfisher perched on an overhanging bough looking hopefully into a deep pool. In November the tree seemed alive with siskins and long tailed tits feeding greedily on the seeds. In the old days the alder trees were 'farmed' by the clog sole makers who fashioned the footwear from its wood. What better timber to use for long lasting clogs in a damp climate than that from a tree which grows with its "feet" in water! This path does get quite muddy after rain, however, and so it is at its best on a hot day in late summer with the smell of hay being harvested and the sound of crickets chirping. Their mating calls are an excellent substitute for car fumes and traffic noise on the main roads leading to and from the tourist traps. The well marked route soon reaches Newton Bridge from which a short climb leads past the Parkers Arms with its beer garden and then on into the village. This hostelry is also famous for the quality of its meals which can be eaten outdoors in the summer. There has probably been a settlement here since Roman times as it is on their road from Lancaster through Wigglesworth and then on to York. There are no remains of this settlement though and neither is there a church – it is close enough to be in the parish of Slaidburn. There is however an historic Quaker's Meeting House built in 1767 and where Newtons' residents once educated their sons thanks to the generosity of John Brabin, a philanthropist from Chipping.

John Bright the politician who was so influential in

repealing the Corn Laws in the 1830s was a pupil of the Quaker school. As the road climbs out of Newton the meeting house is on the right and the burial ground fringed by trees is on the left. This road leads back to Slaidburn by eventually following the line of Croasdale Beck via Laythams. The whole journey can be covered in a short day with a break for lunch and without raising too much of a sweat.

Newton Bridge, with the Parkers Arms in the background. This is another of the excellent hostelries in Bowland.

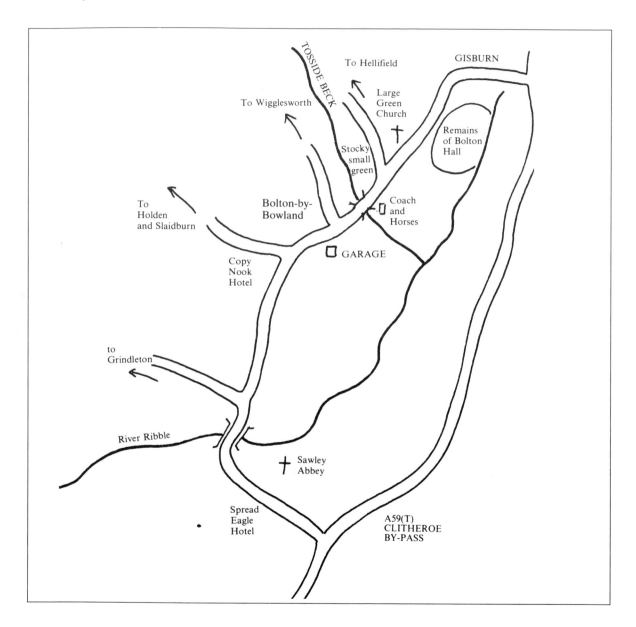

Walk Seven
Bolton by Bowland

ACCESS:

From the A59 Blackburn to Skipton road pass the signs for Whalley, Clitheroe and Chatburn. Turn left at the signs for Sawley. At Sawley cross the bridge over the Ribble after passing the abbey on the right and turning sharp left at the Spread Eagle. Immediately over the bridge turn right and follow the signs for Bolton-by-Bowland.

THE ROUTE:

In recent years the Coach and Horses in the village has become famous for its bar snacks. We try to plan a morning stroll down through the grounds of Bolton Hall situated opposite the church. After lunch in the Coach and Horses we follow the field path to Sawley. This is indicated close to a bridge on the outskirts of the village on the way to the Copy Nook hotel. Follow the path to Sawley, across the rich meadows and return to Bolton-by-Bowland along the narrow road. Pass the Copy Nook on the left. Here is a typical country Inn which has obviously developed from a farm, the old outbuildings still recognisable from the car park. The Inn trade developed as the farmer sold his surplus ale which he brewed himself and provided meals for the weary traveller. This is still the case and the Copy Nook also has a varied menu of bar snacks. From the Copy Nook the road bears right and returns to Bolton-by-Bowland.

*Pendle from
Bolton-by-Bowland*

OUR WALK:

Rain pelted down from an iron grey sky and swept down from
the church into the usually peaceful village of Bolton-by-Bowland.
How can we forget our first visit some years ago when weather
and the harriers of hares shattered the peace? Steam rose from
horses, cold wet hunters reached down from the saddle to pick
up their stirrup cups brimming with warming beverage, dogs
howled and demanded to be off. This was more like 'Hark to fifty
Bountys'. Soon the huntsman gathered his pack and off they set
into the fields around the village. We hoped the brown hares'
long black tipped ears got fair warning of their coming and
galloped away. The sight of a hunt with lovely dogs and horses,
the red and black coats of the hunters and the stirring sound of
the horn is exciting. What a shame it has to end with a killing.
Would not a drag hunt be just as exciting? In this the dogs
chase a trail of aniseed laid by the huntsman.

Since that time we have come to love the peace and tranquillity of the village and the stroll across the fields to Sawley with the ruins of its Cistercian Abbey. Bolton-by-Bowland has two village greens and on the smaller of which, opposite the Coach and Horses Inn has a finely preserved set of stocks. To reach the second green follow the road to Gisburn, but be sure to pause to look at the magnificent church of St Peter and St Paul on the left. The church mainly dates from the 13th century although there was at least one building on the site prior to this date. It is the tower, although it was rebuilt in 1852, which provides students of architecture with most food for thought because it is so different from the normal design seen in these parts. The reason may well be that King Henry VIth spent some time in hiding at Bolton Hall as the guest of his loyal servant Sir Ralph Pudsay. Henry's army had been routed at Hexham in Northumberland in 1464 and the King was obliged to flee. At this time Sir Ralph was rebuilding the church and it is thought that the monarch influenced the design of the tower which shows similarities to those in Somerset with which Henry was certainly familiar. The unfortunate monarch was later captured whilst crossing the River Ribble near Clitheroe and was taken to London where he died. In the grounds of Bolton Hall there is

The Huntsman with his magnificent hounds at Bolton-by-Bowland

also King Henry's well which he used as his open air bathing pool. Alas the once fine hall was demolished earlier this century but the gateposts can still be seen opposite the church and on either side of the track leading down to the river the remnants of the once famous gardens. Sir Ralph has a more permanent record of his efforts on display in the church for here is a memorial slab to the fertile knight, his three wives and twenty five children!

The village itself dominated the area for centuries and in the reign of Edward III (1327-1377) a market charter was granted, and much of eastern Bowland was governed from here. Beyond the church is the second, and by far the largest of the two greens. The side nearest the road is fringed with trees whilst the centre section of the row of buildings opposite is the old courthouse on the roof of which is a weather vane in the shape of a fox. Although this green looks the most impressive it is doubtless the smaller one which is the oldest since here are the stocks and the stump of what was probably the old market cross. In the Domesday Book the village was listed as Bodeton and later as Bolton-juxta-Bowland which is a very accurate description for a settlement on the edge of Bowland Forest and also on the fringe of Ribblesdale. A series of lovely walks from the village lead into both these attractive areas. It is almost but thankfully not quite, possible to follow the route taken by the eccentric William Pudsay who, fleeing from the authority of Elizabeth lst, is reputed to have jumped his horse from a high cliff and over the River Ribble and made good his escape. The tale which is told to explain what has become known as Pudsay's Leap is obviously an intricate weave of a weft of fact but with a more substantial warp of fiction! Whilst on the brink of bankruptcy William was riding in the forest when he met a group of 'little people' who gave him a magic bit for his horse and also told the whereabouts of a rich vein of silver. William quickly restored his

In 1905 Bolton Hall had one of the finest palm houses in Britain. What a tourist attraction it would have made if it was still standing.

fortunes by minting his own coins but Queen Elizabeth on hearing about this was far from amused. The story continues by relating William's escape and his horse protected by the magic bit jumped the impossible gorge across the Ribble and made his way to London. He did have some influence with the Queen who was his godmother but although he kept his head on his shoulders his mines, which were probably in the Rimington area, were confiscated. Not all the tale is fictitious however, because several of the Pudsay shillings marked with an escallop and which William minted are still to be seen in collections.

The stocks at
Bolton-by-Bowland

Whenever we visit Bolton-by-Bowland we think of that first occasion when the rain swept down and the hunt gathered, but whilst writing this chapter we were more fortunate. The autumn day had been hot and the hedgerows were ablaze with colour from rowan, hawthorn and rose fruits. We had collected a couple of pounds of sloes from the blackthorn trees and were thinking of brewing our sloe gin which would keep us warm on many a winter's walk. It was dark when we reached the car and we had not realised that the real excitement of the day was yet to come. We had just passed the cosy old pub, the Copy Nook, when we had to brake hard as a sika deer stag stood defiantly in the centre of the road no doubt dazzled by the headlights. Bowland has always been famous for its deer and it was smashing to see such a splendid stag, but we could not help hoping that the native red deer will sometime return to its old haunts. The Japanese Sika was introduced into Britain in the 19th century as a park animal and the present Bowland animals are probably the remnants of a herd kept by Lord Ribblesdale at Gisburne Park. If we can't have the red then the delightfully alert sikas can be sure of a welcome in our list of the wildlife of Bowland.

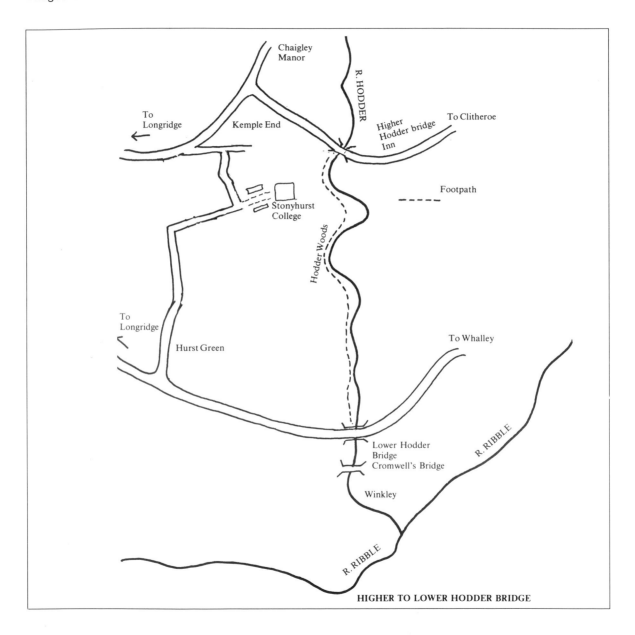

HIGHER TO LOWER HODDER BRIDGE

Walk Eight
Bridges over the Hodder

ACCESS:

Leave Whalley on the Clitheroe road. At the old Grammar school take left along the road to Mitton. Cross the Ribble just beyond the Aspinall Arms on the right, pass through Great Mitton with its church on the right and the Three Fishes Inn on the left. Proceed to cross roads. Follow straight ahead signed Trough of Bowland. Continue to next cross roads and turn left. Pass Higher Hodder Bridge on the right and descend to small parking area close to Higher Hodder bridge.

THE ROUTE:

This is a linear walk which connects three lovely bridges. From the parking place, cross the bridge at the end of which the footpath is signed left. Descend a set of stone steps and then cross a number of wooden footbridges before climbing into the often muddy woodland. At a choice of path take the upper path on the outward journey leaving the lower path to be explored on the return journey. The paths meet close to a wooden footbridge and a stile. Negotiate these and continue along a field path to Lower Hodder bridge. This is a modern road bridge. Cross the often busy road and continue to the ancient bridge known as Cromwell's bridge. This is the end point of the stroll and it is necessary to retrace your steps to the Higher Hodder bridge remembering to keep to the lower path through the woodland.

OUR WALK:

Bowland's largest river, the Hodder, widens and deepens until it

joins the Ribble close to the pleasant village of Hurst Green between Whalley and Longridge. A delightful and well signed walk begins at Higher Hodder bridge below the Inn of the same name and twists along an undulating route to Lower Hodder bridge and the river's confluence with the Ribble. Most of the path passes through tangled trees and drifts of flowers and Hodder Woods have been known and loved by naturalists for many years. It is not just local folk who know the woods thanks to the works of the poet Gerard Manley Hopkins (1844-1889). This shy man was a Jesuit teacher at the nearby Stonyhurst College who found perhaps the only real peace in his life during his wanderings through Hodder Woods. The surrounding hills were also well known to the poet who wrote about the kestrel thus:

The Windhover
To Christ our Lord

I caught this mornings minion, kingdom of daylight's dauphin,
dapple-dawn-dawn Falcon, in his riding
Of the rolling level underneath his steady air, and striding high
there, how he rung upon the rein of a wimpling wing
In his ecstasy! then off, off forth on swing.
As a skate's heel sweeps smooth on a bowbend: the hurl and
gliding
Rebuffed the big wind. My heart in hiding
Stirred for a bird, the achieve of, the mastery of the
thing!
Brute beauty and valour and act, oh, air, pride, plume, here
Buckle! AND the fire that breaks from the thee then, a billion
Times told lovelier, more dangerous, O my chevalier!
No wonder of it: sheer plod makes plough down sillion
Shine, and blueblcak ombere, ah my dear,
Fall, gall themselves, and gash goldvermillion.

Whilst we find some of the language used by Hopkins a

Facing page:
The otter is still occasionally found around both the Hodder and the Ribble of which it is a tributary.

63

little difficult we know of no other poet who captures the atmosphere of the Hodder valley so well.

Our own fondest memory of Hodder woods takes us back to early dawn on a beautifully gentle spring morning whilst we were preparing to record a radio programme of the dawn chorus. Blackbird, song thrush, robin, wren and willow warbler were all soon in full song and as the pink flush of dawn crept through the trees a sleepy sounding tawny owl joined in sounding, we thought, a little sad that the hunting night was over. Above the surrounding fields a curlew's bubbling call blended with the soaring notes of the skylark. Soon the morning light revealed the full glory of a bluebell wood filled with an azure mist and heavy scent. Dotted among the sea of blue were the white star like heads of ramsons which looked like jewels and smelled like garlic!

Kingfisher, dipper and grey wagtail are resident along this stretch of river and we are always sorry when we reach Lower Hodder bridge and meet up with the modern world speeding along the Longridge to Whalley road. For a lover of bridges, however there is some consolation for here are two spans. Standing on one bridge it is possible to look downstream at a splendidly proportioned packhorse bridge built in 1562 by Richard Shireburn at a cost of £70. Locals refer to this as Cromwell's Bridge in the belief that the Protector stayed at the Shireburn's mansion at Stonyhurst in August 1648 and marched his army over the bridge. It is, however, a narrow bridge for a large army and its cumbersome ordnance and luggage and it is much more likely that the Hodder was forded at a point close to the meeting with the Ribble at Winckley.

To discover what happened to the Shireburn family and their mansion of Stonyhurst we must take a look at the village of Hurst Green turning right at the Shireburn Arms. To the right is a row of Alms houses looking as if they had been there for centuries. If you read the inscription you see that they were built in 1706 at Kemple End some $3^{1}/_{2}$ miles away and close to

the Higher Hodder bridge! In 1946 they were carefully removed and reassembled for the use of workers employed by the school. Few stately homes in the North of England have fared so well as Stonyhurst despite it having such an unlucky start. Whilst Sir Nicholas Shireburn was watching his new house being built his young and only son died after having eaten yew berries. Nicholas died in 1717 and his daughter who was married to the Duke of Norfolk, a prominent Catholic supporter, inherited the estate. After the death of the Duchess of Norfolk, Stonyhurst came into the hands of Thomas Weld who, in 1794, leased the house to a teaching order – the Jesuits. Thomas Weld's son, also called Thomas became a Cardinal and the future of the school was thus assured and has thrived ever since. Stonyhurst has a long tradition of academic excellence and famous old scholars include the actor Charles Laughton and Sir Arthur Conan Doyle. Some experts have suggested that the *Hound of the Baskervilles* may have been based on the mists which sometimes clothe the hills of

Higher Hodder Bridge photographed in 1905

The old packhorse bridge, often called Cromwell's Bridge photographed from the Lower Hodder Bridge

East Lancashire, but he must also have known its more gentle side.

We have often sat among the bilberries and heather around Kemple End listening to the June cuckoo, the male calling without apparent pause for breath, whilst his silent mate seeks out the nest of a meadow pipit in which to slyly slip her egg for the host to incubate and then struggle to feed the comparatively huge infant. We also remember the same spot on breezy April mornings when the first wheatears of the year flit among the stone walls and their white rumps flash in the sunlight. Kemple End has the rugged grandeur typical of Northern moorlands and yet its wilderness is tempered by the presence of cosy hotels and villages with smoke rising in spirals from the chimneys of the cottages.

This is something of a contrast to the windswept heights of the Trough of Bowland which blocks the opposite end of the Hodder valley.

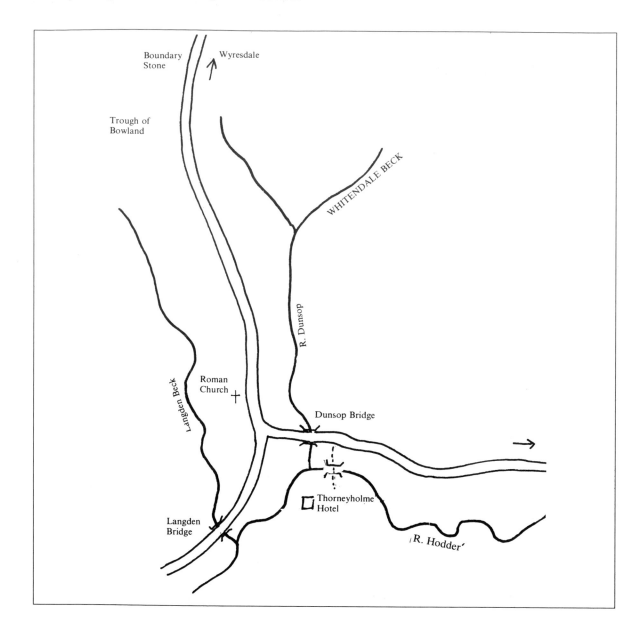

Walk Nine

Dunsop Bridge and the Trough of Bowland

ACCESS:

From Clitheroe and Whalley follow the signs for the Trough of Bowland passing Browsholme Hall on the left and passing through Whitewell and into Dunsop Bridge.

ROUTE:

Footpaths in Bowland have not been well marked but things are steadily improving and the three strolls described here are all obviously marked. Only the walk up to the Trough of Bowland boundary stone is at all strenuous, but this can be reached by car and there is some parking space at the head of the pass.

OUR WALKS:

We once sat quietly eating a cream tea in the lounge of the Thorneyholme Hotel looking out into the gardens and watching the raindrops reflecting the rays of the afternoon sun. After the shower came the heat and the steam of water vapour evaporating from the well-tended lawns carried the scent of newly cut grass. From Dunsop Bridge car park there are three possible strolls. Two follow the course of the River Hodder. The path downstream leads to Whitewell, whilst an equally pleasant route upstream leads to Newton.

The third crosses a bridge over the river, through the village of Dunsop Bridge and then up to the famous Trough of Bowland with its splendidly savage scenery. We can never resist a short stroll downstream to the point where the River Dunsop merges with the Hodder. There is no finer river scenery anywhere than this. A common sandpiper called to its young which were hiding under the umbrella-like leaves of a butterbur, and trout were leaping out of the deep pools to catch the insects on the clear surface of the water.

The Towneley family of Burnley had strong connections with Dunsop Bridge, and the old stables at Thorneyholme housed many of the family's horses and their fine cattle have grazed the fields around these parts for centuries. The most famous of all the animals was the racehorse *Kettledrum* which won the 1861 Derby at the long odds of 16-1.

All the locals seem to have benefitted and it is said that St. Hubert's church, sited on the left of the road from Dunsop Bridge into the Trough of Bowland, was financed by the winnings. The church, consecrated in 1865, is Roman Catholic as we would expect as it is connected with the Towneleys.

Dunsop Bridge is a favourite spot with paddlers, picnickers and gentle strollers.

70

St. Hubert's church situated on the left of the road from Dunsop Bridge to the Trough of Bowland.

Kettledrum was trained at Stud Farm and the dark chestnut stallion with three white stockings was famous for miles around.

The whole of Dunsop appears to have been one huge stud farm and although one fascinating set of stables on the site of the present trout hatchery has long been demolished, others of equally impressive dimensions remain. Apparently, there was even a horse bath in one of the boxes long before the majority of houses had such luxury! There were also small holes in the doors so that grooms could inspect their valuable charges without disturbing them.

The local roads must always have been busy with important traffic and at the junction of the road into Dunsop Bridge is the original finger signpost dated 1739 which tells us that Clitheroe is seven miles, Lancaster 11 miles and Hornby 10 miles, whilst the distance to Slaidburn has been eroded by the weather. The modern signpost over it disputes the distances and

See how the pheasant contrasts with the lush vegetation.

the spelling by listing Slaidburn as four miles, Clitheroe at 11 and reflecting the decline in the influence of Hornby by not mentioning it at all.

Lancaster via the Trough of Bowland is given as $14^{1}/_{2}$ miles and it was this road that we chose to drive up slowly. At the end of the day, we picnicked at the boundary stone at the head of the pass. This marks the junction of the old counties of Lancashire and Yorkshire before the boundaries were altered in 1974.

After finishing our meal, we enjoyed the steep descent alongside Langden Beck which, like the Dunsop, joins the Hodder but not before giving up most of its catchment to the water board. In the summer there are several suitable pull-ins, one on the right having kiosks selling ice cream and hot snacks.

Despite the loss of many trees from Tudor times onwards a considerable amount of planting took place in the early 19th century when Fenton-Cawthorne purchased 1,500 acres of land on both sides of the Trough summit. On the Yorkshire side a great deal of lime burning took place, but shelterbeds of pines and other conifers were planted for game and sheep. Red grouse are still common here and sheep wandering across the road are a constant hazard to traffic.

From his vantage point at Wyresdale Tower, Fenton looked down into Lancashire. From the boundary stone the route of the small tributaries to the Hodder can be seen on the Bowland side. A look to the west reveals a panoramic view of the River Wyre. But this is another route to be saved and savoured for another day. Wyresdale, especially Abbeystead, has a charm all of its own!

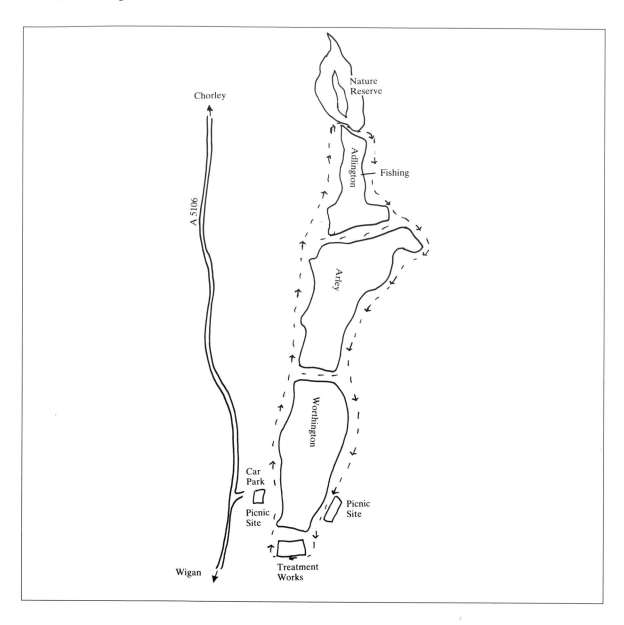

Walk Ten
Around Worthington Lakes

ACCESS:

Worthington is situated between Chorley and Wigan near Standish and just off the A49, one of the earliest Turnpike Roads in Lancashire. Keep a sharp look out and you will find many of the original iron milemarkers still in position. Those approaching from Chorley will pass the White Crow Inn on the left about a mile before the sign for Worthington Lakes. Those approaching from Wigan should not fail to visit the White Crow either before or after their walk around "The Lakes" because it opens all day and provides substantial bar snacks. There is an extensive car park, lots of picnic tables, an Information Centre, cafe and a classroom which schools can hire for the day. Dog owners may take exception to the fact that dogs are not welcome on the walks. Our labrador was no doubt disappointed but as Worthington Lakes provide drinking water, only the foolish and irresponsible owners would object.

THE ROUTE:

From the car park proceed forward towards the reservoir and then bear left to the Information Centre. The well marked route follows the shoreline of three reservoirs and around the edge of a conservation area before swinging around and following the opposite bank. After crossing several fields swing right, pass under the water tower and return to the car park.

The White Crow, situated close to Worthington Lakes, is a good place to enjoy a meal before or after your walk.

OUR WALK:

There are three reservoirs here fed by two substantial streams, but an even larger river flows beneath the lakes. During the construction in the late 19th century of Worthington, Arley and Adlington reservoirs , the River Douglas was actually culverted and flows beneath them. Adlington provides water for a bleach works whilst Worthington and Arley provide drinking water for the Wigan area. There is a water treatment works at the lower end and this can filter and chlorinate up to 4 million gallons per day after which it is pumped to a covered storage reservoir which is only $1\frac{1}{2}$ miles away at Prospect.

Since 1977 Worthington has functioned as a small country park and fishing is allowed. On Worthington, anglers catch trout, barbel, rudd, roach and perch. On Arley there are barbel, carp, tench, bream and roach; whilst Arlington has carp, bream, tench, roach, perch and gudgeon.

We were lucky on our last visit to the lakes as we met one of the wardens who was busy catching goldfinches in a cunning little trap baited with seeds which the delightful birds find irresistible. The warden took us into his laboratory and we watched him ring the birds, weigh and measure them. Each bird weighed between 15 and 20 grams. When you think that there are about 28 grams to one ounce, then 5 goldfinches weigh the same as a quarter of sweets! They are released unharmed.

We had only just begun our tour of the lakes when we saw a pair of great crested grebes doing a spot of courting. One bird, presumably the male, carried a bunch of water weed up to his mate and then dived in front of her only to emerge a few seconds later still carrying the weed in his bill. He presented her with the posy and many scientists think that this present is a sort of engagement ring to cement the two as a breeding pair. Great crested grebes have recovered from near extinction less than 100 years ago, when they were hunted because of their beautifully coloured feathers.

Those who feel that an area sandwiched between Wigan and Chorley cannot be either pretty or of interest to naturalists should not be misled for here is a nature reserve to rival any deep in open countryside. Roe deer wander around the wooded areas fringing the reservoirs and other common mammals include rabbit, grey squirrel, long tailed field mouse, bank vole and both stoat and weasel.

Our lasting memory, however, was of the goldfinches as we have never seen so many together in a flock and we were impressed with how gently they were trapped, ringed and released. Ringing tells us how long birds live, how far they travel and how they meet their deaths. Each ring bears a

One of the beautifully restored milestones on the old Turnpike road between Wigan and Chorley.

The water tower at Worthington Lakes.

unique number and the address of the British Trust for Ornithology who co-ordinate the programme in England. Scientists throughout the world are in contact with each other and even during the last war ring numbers were exchanged between England and Germany via Ireland and in the diplomatic bag. The professional scientists could not hope to ring enough birds to discover details of their lives and rely on amateur ringers at places such as Worthington Lakes to provide them with data. The "amateurs" have skills which many professionals envy and the amateurs also have all the fun – what a joy it. is to handle such beautiful little creatures.

Worthington Lakes provide a delightful and gentle walk just for the scenery but the fact that such important ornithological research is going on is an added bonus which adds spice to the stroll.

A goldfinch being handled gently prior to being ringed at Worthington Lakes.

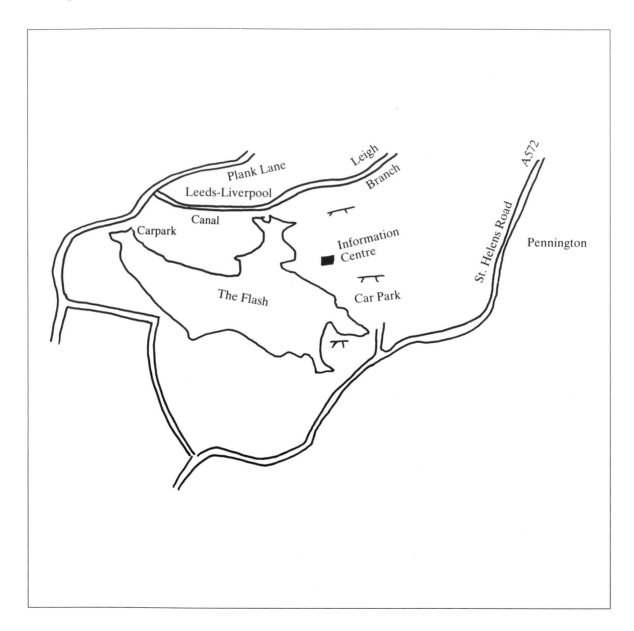

Walk Eleven
Pennington Flash

ACCESS:
The main entrance to the flash, which has a spacious car park overlooking the water, is off the A572 St Helens road in the vicinity of its junction with the recently constructed Leigh By-Pass.

THE ROUTE:
The well signed circular path around the flash is around 2 miles and around 2 to 3 hours should be allowed for the stroll. There are several places to rest including some well sited hides.

OUR WALK:
Pennington flash is an area of 170 acres of water one mile to the south west of Leigh and since 1981 it has been incorporated into a country park which exceeds 1,000 acres. At one time the area was entirely devoted to agriculture, the low lying fields being split by the meanderings of Hey Brook. Once the Leeds to Liverpool canal had been constructed towards the end of the 18th century a branch was cut to Leigh; this now constitutes the northern extremity of the park and overlooks Bickershaw colliery which was one of the reasons for the canal branch being cut. Extensive mining particularly prior to nationalisation led to subsidence and flooding. Wildfowl and other marsh birds are never slow to take advantage of such ideal habitat, but their populations were initially kept at low levels by the uncontrolled activities of local shooters. Thanks to firm but understanding wardening, shooting has been very much reduced and wildfowl

Pennington Flash in winter and overlooked by the old spoil heaps of Bickershaw Colliery.

numbers are increasing in consequence. This also adds to the enjoyment of the walk. Ambitious landscaping of old spoil heaps and associated mine railway tracks has produced a variety of other habitats, especially native hardwoods such as birch, oak and ash but there are also some stands of conifers. As they mature such areas are bound to increase the variety of species found around the edge of the water. Under the trees interesting fungi grow including ink cap, sulphur tuft, orange peel, razor strop and candle snuff.

The Ink Cap Fungus is one of the many species of fungus growing in the wooded areas overlooking the flash. The wooded areas are maturing quickly.

On the Flash itself anglers and boating interests have both been catered for, but areas of shallow water and reed beds have been reserved for the birds and are carefully protected. Encouraged by the chance of a good day's watching from well sited hides increasing numbers of good ornithologists are visiting the flash and little now escapes their sharp eyes. The Dalmatian pelican spotted in August 1970 was not accepted as a new British record as it was doubtless an escape from a collection.

There is an Information Centre providing exhibits and details of the footpaths which run through the park and afford views over stretches of water including the well named Grebe Lodge which is a popular haven for both little and great crested grebe especially when sailing is taking place on the open stretches. Little grebe are also known as dabchicks – some 10 to 12 pairs now breeding at Pennington; the winter population is much higher but often declines dramatically during adverse winters. J.D. Wilson pointed out that local dabchicks have developed nocturnal habits by moving down Pennington Brook which is often illuminated by the lights of an adjacent urban conurbation. There are usually between 5 and 8 pairs of great crested grebes plus around 25 non-breeding individuals which summer on the flash. In the autumn they are joined by birds from other areas numbers usually peaking during October with the 87 recorded on 12 October 1980 being the then county record for Lancashire. After this initial concentration numbers decline as the winter progresses and this suggests that Pennington may be a post breeding collecting point and from which birds spread out to other stretches of water in the surrounding district including Scotsman's Flash at Wigan and Lightshaw Flash at Leigh. A low ebb of between 15 and 20 birds is reached in the depths of winter but rises again to around 40 between March and May. There have also been summer sightings of black necked grebes which has led to speculation of breeding.

Some species have been attracted by careful planning but others have arrived uninvited. In order to produce scrapes suitable for waders it was necessary to lower the water levels, and in an area evocatively named Sorrowcow Farm old tree stumps were exposed. These have proved ideal perches for cormorants which are thought to belong to the continental race *Phalocrocorax carbo sinensis*. Fishermen – sometimes understandably – object to their presence especially when the winter population approaches 80 birds. The more marine based shag is not often recorded but there was a single bird present during the last two months of 1980 and suffering from having swallowed a discarded fishing line.

The exclusion of visitors from parts of the flash has allowed wigeon to graze throughout the winter, especially in hard weather and feeding flocks of around 80 are now common. Breeding in the not too distant future is a distinct possibility. On July 1st 1979 a female shelduck with three downy young was seen on the Hey Brook approach to the flash. It was not known

The little grebe was among the first species of bird to take advantage of the Country Park.

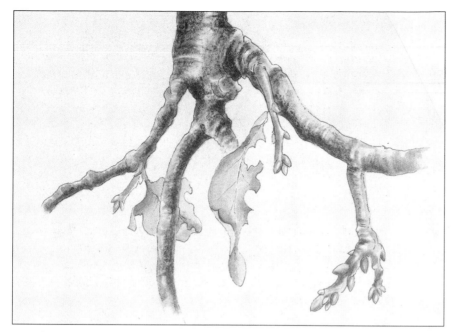

The oak seedlings planted around Pennington Flash are now developing well.

at the time whether the nest site was at Pennington or Lightshaw; further breeding successes in l980, l981 and 1983 and in the early 1990's have indicated that Lightshaw is the likely site.

Perhaps the most worrying feature of the 1980s flash was the failure of the mute swan to breed successfully. It really ought to be a regular breeder but the fact that it is not is due to the attentions of vandals and perhaps the sheer presence – albeit innocent – of anglers. In the past the effect of lead shot cannot be discounted. Since lead shot was replaced by a plastic alternative the swan population have increased dramatically and Pennington will soon be a regular breeding site.

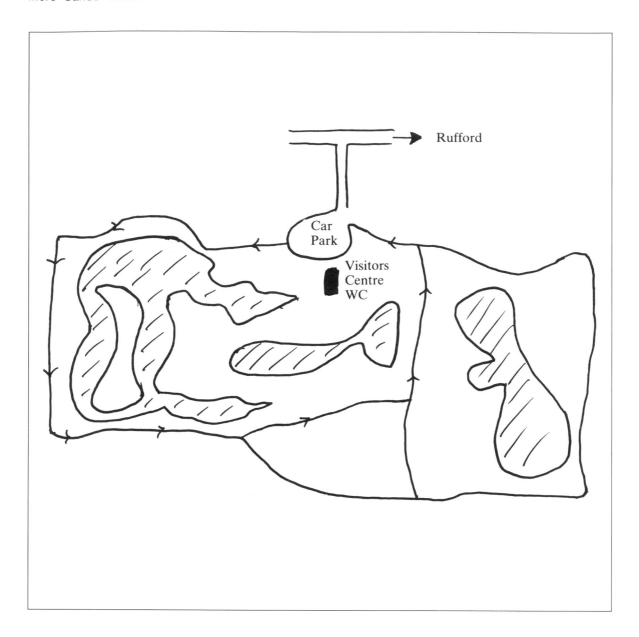

Walk Twelve
Mere Sands Wood

ACCESS:

This nature reserve is overshadowed by its much larger near neighbour Martin Mere run by the Wildfowl and Wetlands Trust but both have a vital rôle to play. Mere Sands is run by the Lancashire Trust for Nature Conservation. From the A59 Preston to Liverpool road at Rufford turn right and follow the signs for Martin Mere. Drive slowly and keep a look out to the left as you travel along a straight road. Mere Sands Wood is signed to the left and is close to a residential kennels for dogs. There is a small car park, book shop and Information Centre for which a small fee is required. Entry on Sundays is restricted to members of the Trust who are also admitted free. Membership is available at the Centre. Dogs are welcome but should be kept on lead.

THE ROUTE:

From the car park turn left along a circular nature trail allowing ample time to enter each of the several hides on the route overlooking the pools which are the flooded workings of a disused sand quarry, the whole area occupying about 100 acres (40 hectares). There are several choices which can vary the length of the flat walk, but this is a level track through mixed woodland screening the shallow pools.

OUR WALK:

We always try to walk nature trails at least four times so that we can compare the seasons. The last time we walked this route

87

was just before Easter and we were rewarded almost immediately by the sight of a pair of red squirrels chasing each other through the trees. One of the animals was so dark that he seemed almost black. To find red squirrels in Lancashire is something of a rarity these days as they died out long ago and have been replaced by the larger and more aggressive grey squirrel which was introduced from North America in the 1870s. Other mammals recorded in the woodland include bank vole, stoat, pipistrelle and noctule bats whilst on a January evening we watched a red fox slinking about in the undergrowth which is dominated by rhododendron which seems to be being controlled by the wardens.

It is the bird hides which attract most visitors and they are all reached by paths which are almost all dry and any wet areas are usually spanned by stoutly constructed wooden bridges. The bird list is impressive but being close to the coast sea ducks are often in evidence especially shelduck, wigeon and the occasional red breasted merganser. Fresh water species are also in evidence including the ubiquitous mallard, tufted duck, teal and pochard plus both great crested and little grebe. The water is fringed by reeds and overhung with vegetation dominated by willow, alder, birch, gorse and of course rhododendron, the latter two providing cover for common breeding birds such as finches, thrushes, robin and hedge sparrow. The tangle of bramble provides nest sites for blackcap, willow warbler and cover for shelduck and the common partridge. At all times of the year the woodland seems to echo to the piping notes of pheasants.

We have seldom walked around Mere Sands in the afternoon without passing families with young children some on their first ever birdwatching trip which they will never forget. Those who consider themselves "serious" birdwatchers should come early or stay late. Better still they should join the children and be surprised how quickly young eyes learn to spot the birds.

Facing page: A melanistic (black) squirrel is a very rare variety indeed

*At Mere Sands is
one of the finest
hides we have ever
seen*

One of the reed-fringed lakes formed as the old sand quarries flooded.

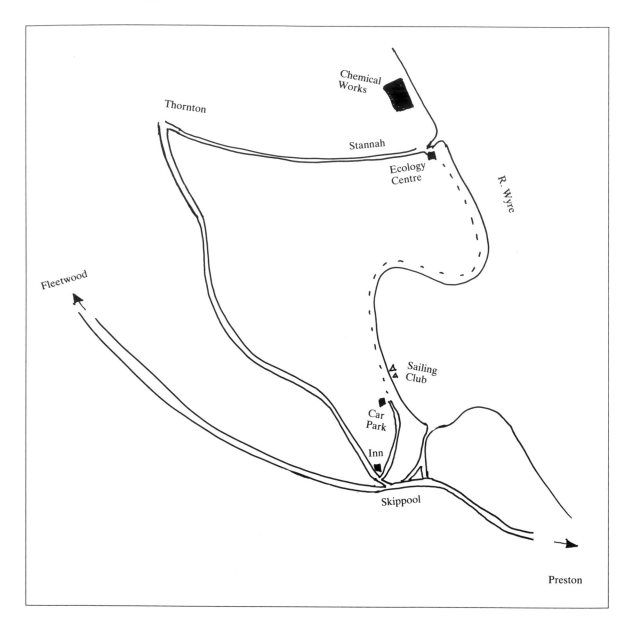

Walk Thirteen

Around Poulton, Skippool and Stanah

ACCESS:

From Preston follow the M55 and then follow the signs for Fleetwood. (A585) Poulton is signed from this road. To reach Skippool return to the A585 and continue to Skippool. The Creek is signed left off the main road and then immediately right. Descend the narrow track to the car park on the left. If you wish to start from Stanah do not turn right to the Creek but continue straight ahead until you see brown signs indicating Stanah and its Ecology Centre.

ROUTE:

This is another linear walk which can be done either from Skippool or from Stanah where there are good toilet facilities. The distance between the two is just over $1^1/_2$ miles which means that the whole stroll can easily be covered in three hours allowing plenty of time for birdwatching along the hedgerows and over the estuary. From Skippool car park turn left and follow the road alongside the creeks and from which there are good views across the Wyre to the Toll Bridge. Bear left and pass the boat club following the obvious coastal path.

OUR WALK:

The River Wyre has long been one of our favourite rivers. In recent years a nature trail has opened along the river bank between Skippool and the Wyreside Ecology Centre at Stanah, a distance of $1^3/_4$ miles which makes a splendid walk with a picnic

93

Poulton-le-Fylde's Church of St. Chad is a pretty picture during March when the crocuses are in full bloom

lunch prior to returning. Half way between the two is a picnic site at Cockle Hall.

The word Skippool comes from the Saxon word Skiff which means a small boat. In the 16th century the Wyre estuary was used by shipping which sheltered in harbours on both sides of the river. On a delightfully sunny morning we stood at Skippool and looked across the incoming tide to Wardleys.

At one time Skippool Creek was navigable as far as Poulton-le-Fylde which was a port second in importance in the north west only to Chester around 1700. In 1708 a Customs House was opened with William Jennings appointed as its officer on the then large salary of £30 per annum. By the mid 1700s Poulton, Skippool and Wardleys handled more cargo than Liverpool and imports included wines, spirits, tobacco, sugar, rum, cotton, oranges and timber from America, West Indies and Russia. Guano was also brought in from South West Africa to enrich the farmlands of the Fylde.

Although almost swamped by the Blackpool conurbation, Poulton has more than a trace of its medieval past with a set of

94

stocks, market cross and a whipping post overlooking the pedestrianised old market square behind which is the parish church of St Chad which has been on this site since Norman times, but the present building only dates to the 17th century with a great deal of Georgian reconstruction including the splendid gallery.

The arrival of the railway at Fleetwood around 1840 reduced the trade reaching the riverside ports to a trickle, but Wardley and Skippool were already experiencing problems as the boats increased in size at the time that the river was silting. The narrow creeks are these days busier than they have been for

The stocks, whipping post, pedestrianised centre and parish church at Poulton-le-Fylde

many years and provide safe anchorage for private motor cruisers and yachts. This is also wonderful birdwatching country and the mudflats provide feeding grounds for dunlin, knot, redshank and sanderling. Teal and shelduck roost and feed on the salt marshes. The footpath to Stanah is flat and well maintained and becoming increasingly popular with naturalists. The site now occupied by Stanah car park and the Wyresdale Ecology Centre was once a rubbish tip but the salt marsh has been restored with hardly a scar to be seen. The centre provides clean toilets and well appointed Information Centre. Visitors can launch their boats into the estuary from a slip way from the car park. This is a splendid stretch of river despite being overlooked by the ICI industrial complex of Hillhouse International which blends surprisingly well into the scenery. Mining for rock salt began in 1892 but the methods used these days are much more sophisticated and involve running water onto the underground salt deposits. The dissolved brine is then pumped to the surface. This is now used in the manufacture of polymers and so here we have industry and wildlife in perfect harmony and we have to admit that we need both in this modern age.

Facing page: Skippool is a complex of tidal creeks full of boats

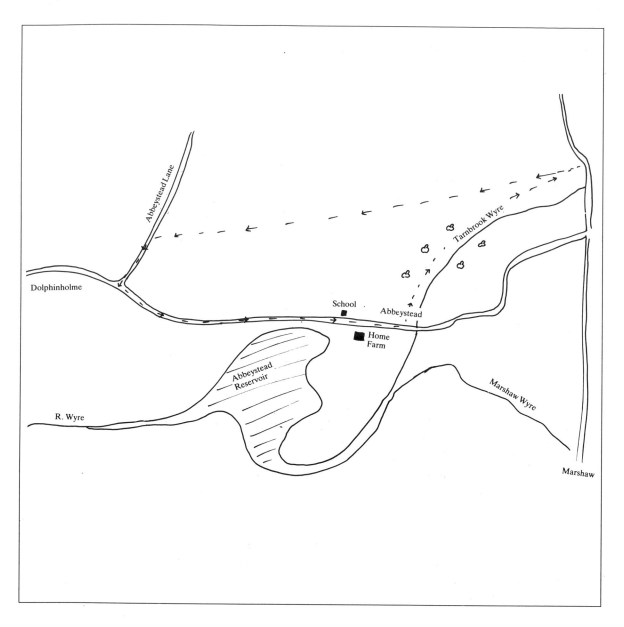

Walk Fourteen

Abbeystead and The Wyre

ACCESS:

From the A6 road between Lancaster and Preston the Trough of Bowland is signed. Abbeystead is reached via Dolphinholme. There is limited parking in the usually quiet and always beautiful village. It can also be reached from Dunsop Bridge by travelling over the Trough of Bowland (see walk no. 9).

ROUTE:

From the school follow the road towards the Trough of Bowland. A footpath is then taken to the left which follows the Tarnbrook Wyre. There is a pleasant little copse on the left. At the road turn left and then left again at a gate. Cross the fields until you meet a track called Abbeystead Lane. Turn left at the end of this and then left at the main road to return to the village.

OUR WALK:

Wyresdale is one of the unsung valleys of England and it is difficult to understand why. The river has two sources, both rising on the mossy slopes of the Trough of Bowland. These are the Tarnbrook and the Marshaw Wyre, and around them breed redshank and curlew, snipe and that lovely little relative of the linnet, the twite. The male twite which is resident here has a pink rump, which contrasts with the startlingly white rump of the summer visiting wheatear which is with us from April to October. These two unpolluted streams flow through tree-lined cloughs which provide food and shelter for large numbers of

sheep. They meet near Abbeystead, at a spot called Emmott. The name indicates that at one time monks were settled at their Abbey Stead, and this made good sense because this is ideal sheep country. A group of Cistercian monks made an attempt to establish an abbey here but apparently found the climate too tough – there are often very heavy snow falls in winter – and decided to try their luck in Ireland, where they found Wythney much more to their liking.

*Facing page:
Abbeystead and
the Tarnbrook
Wyre*

Apart from sheep, the moors are the home of the red grouse. The land, now part of the Westminster estates, has often been walked by royalty in search of a fat brace of grouse. In summer the guttural grouse call, which sounds like "go back, go back", mingles with the heavy drone of bees loaded with nectar. Many local farms and cottages have honey for sale, and it has that lovely summer scent of heather and thyme. Also breeding on the heather are the larvae of the delightfully coloured moth, the Emperor.

Abbeystead is set in a dip among sweeping hills and has many fine buildings clustered around the old school. The post office is housed in a building constructed in 1674, its ceilings supported by huge oak beams. There is also an old horse trough, a remnant of the days when travel was a much more leisurely affair, but the real joy of this village is not so much in its stone as in its flowers. It seems to be a riot of colour in every season. No sooner have the last of the roses faded than the leaves of snowdrops are poking their way through the earth. Then come the daffodils and the summer flush of hollyhocks, marigolds, pansies, michaelmas daisies, lupins and the rest. Then there are the wild flowers: the green flowers of dog's mercury, the bright shining yellow petals of lesser celandine, the pale nodding heads of wood anemone and the bluebells blend to illuminate the hedgerows. Later in the year the roses perfume the leafy footpaths and are in turn replaced by the heady scent of

The Marshaw Wyre

honeysuckle. In springtime the wet meadows are carpeted with clumps of marsh marigold. A pleasant walk of about a mile from Abbeystead, along a tree fringed road, leads to Christ's Church over Wyresdale. It gets its local name of the Shepherd's Church from the inscription above the door, which reads "O-Ye Shepherds hear the word of the Lord". The stained glass windows depict scenes from the bible associated with sheep. These are obviously very easy to find but the theme is highly appropriate for a moorland area.

Such a vast catchment area was obviously too valuable to be ignored by planners during the periods of industrial expansion and water has been piped to the northern towns for nearly 100 years. It was one of these pumping stations in which an explosion occurred and caused such grievous loss of life at

Abbeystead in the spring of 1984.

Close to Abbeystead and reached via a footpath is a "lake" through which flows the River Wyre. This stretch of water was constructed to provide compensation water for the river as more and more industries developed along its banks and demanded water. Just downstream, at Dolphinholme, a whole complex of mills was developed, but most of the buildings are now derelict. The workers' cottages, however, are still lived in and on the corner of a wall is a gas lamp bracket. It is said that Dolphinholme was the first place in Britain to try out gas-lit street lamps.

Now that the mills have gone the lake has developed reed beds which are excellent hunting grounds for dragonflies and butterflies, with flowers such as water forget-me-not, bur reed, phragmites, yellow flag and willows. Increasing numbers of birds are both wintering and breeding here, and in the winter of 1984 we watched bearded tits feeding on the seeds of phragmites. This uncommon species is not related to the titmice but belong to a completely different family. It is better to refer to it as the bearded reedling. Its scientific name is *Panurus biamarcus*. It is distinguished by its long tail, which comes in useful when it is balancing on reeds blowing about in the wind. The female is brown above and pale on the underparts, but the cock bird is a very attractive fellow, with a blue-grey head and very obvious black moustache. We doubt whether it will ever breed at Abbeystead but it may well become a regular winter visitor if the reed beds around the "lake" are allowed to develop. The water leaves the lake by cascading over an artificial waterfall which crashes into a leafy dell rich in liverworts and mosses and screened by a curtain of ferns. The designers did not forget the Wyre's salmon and a ladder has been built on the edges to enable the fish to reach the lake.

Abbeystead is one of Wyredale's most beautiful villages,

Facing page:
Salmon Ladder on
the River Wyre
near Abbeystead

but the best way to view the whole valley is to climb Jubilee Tower on the main Dunsop Bridge to Lancaster road. Built to commemorate Queen Victoria's Diamond Jubilee in 1897 the tower has steps leading to a viewing platform from which can be seen the Furness Fells, Lake District mountains, the Fylde coast and beyond to the Mersey estuary. Standing here with the breeze blowing through one's hair it is easy to realise how important the road through the Trough of Bowland once was. In bad weather how welcome villages such as Abbeystead must have been to weary travellers.

Shepherds Church,
Abbeystead

The Crook of Lune

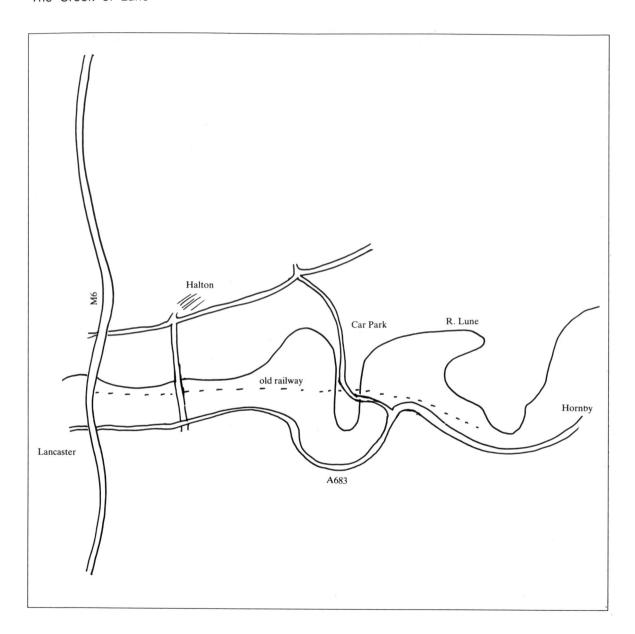

Walk Fifteen
The Crook of Lune

ACCESS:

From Lancaster follow the A683 towards Kirkby Lonsdale and Hornby. Just before Hornby a left turn signed Halton leads to a road crossing the twisting loop of the river and also the old railway line. The car park and toilets are on the right just after the road has ascended and twisted among stout hedgerows.

THE ROUTE:

Being a railway line this is a linear walk but there are several diversions from the path. The best of these is from the old disused station at Halton. Here cross a narrow bridge beneath which anglers fish and after the bridge bear left to explore Halton. After retracing your steps do not return to the car park without a long period standing on the viaduct and enjoying the wonderful views. From the viaduct there is a short well marked walk across fields to another small picnic site overlooking the riverside with impressive views of the road bridge and the viaduct.

OUR WALK:

A lovely name for a lovely sweep of the river 'The Crook of Lune' now has a toilet block, ample parking and picnic tables. The area was so loved by the artist Turner that he painted the scene between 1816 and 1818; in 1835 Wordsworth praised the spot in his "Guide to the Lakes". Then in 1849 came the railway which punched its way up Lunesdale from Green Ayre station at Lancaster to Wennington. It was constructed by the North

The bridge at the Crook of Lune is one of the finest in the country

Western Railway company and was known as the Little North Western to distinguish it from its larger competitor the London North Western Railway which began in 1846. The Luneside company was never very efficient and they had very little rolling stock. They obtained some stock from one Edmund Sharpe, but this was apparently too wide, too low, and too heavy. The width of the doors in particular meant that if they were opened on entry to the station waiting passengers would have been swept away. In 1852 the Midland railway took over, leasing in 1859 and finally buying the line in 1871. In 1923 it became part of

the London Midland and Scottish (LMS) network and remained so until the railways were nationalised. When Dr. Beeching's cuts axed the line in 1966 the route was first closed to passengers and a little later to goods. The lines have gone, the bridges are rusting away, but the magnificent views remain to be enjoyed by walkers since the line has been converted into a footpath.

One section begins at the car park and toilets above the Crook of Lune. A pear tree grows here which we found to be full of small hard fruits. A few leaves remained on the branches as did the odd fruit. The ground beneath was covered in leaves and windfalls. We ate an odd pear which was not as bitter as expected. The temperature was falling quickly and birds were everywhere including chaffinches, bullfinches and a lovely charm of goldfinches feeding on the seeds of thistles. This delightful little acrobat is adept at feeding above ground extracting seeds not only from thistles but also from alder trees both of which grow well around the Crook of Lune. The colourful flickering of black and gold wings and the pied tail may well function as a flag keeping the flock in close contact. After all a group is more likely to be successful in finding food than one bird on its own. Another characteristic of feeding goldfinches is their ability to hold down the food plant with a foot, whilst plucking out the seeds with their thin tapering bills. Its bright colours, simple seed diet and musical song meant that in the 19th century it was a popular cage bird. It did, not, however,live very long in captivity and consequently many thousands of birds were trapped in Victorian England. The decrease was very obvious and in 1888 the trade was made illegal. There was soon a marked increase and apart from being adversely affected by bad winters the population has been gradually increasing to the present level of around 300,000 pairs. Judging by the large numbers of goldfinches moving on this day it seemed to suggest bad weather on the way.

Apart from the option of following the line of the old railway there is a splendid short walk which is signed off to the right from the railway bridge, crossing a lush riverside field, and over the road near the 'motor bridge' to a picnic site above the Lune. The path then follows the meander of the river into a small but delightful woodland rising steeply from the waterside. Here we found several species of fungi including stinkhorn, Jew's ear and honey fungus. The latter grows in groups from the late summer to the longest night or can be found joined at the base to form clusters. It is always attached to old tree trunks, stumps or buried wood, either directly or by its vegetative stage which darkens and aggregates to form strands resembling boot laces. It is a parasite and causes trees to wilt and die. We were once standing in a woodland as it went dark and the honey fungus growing on an old beech glowed with a greenish-white light. To our ancestors here was a goblin of the woods carrying his tiny lantern. Some authorities say that honey fungus is edible but the quality is described as inferior so we don't think we'll ever bother sampling it.

Apart from the fungi, white deadnettle and red campion were still in bloom and fieldfares and redwings were feeding on rosehip, hawthorn and, we think on the black, ripe and surprisingly succulent berries of ivy. Round the bend of the river driven on the current were a dozen mallards, already paired off plus two males and one female goosander.

Close to the Crook of Lune is the delightful village of Halton. St Wilfrid's Church is said to have been founded in the 7th century but is, according to Fleetwood-Hesketh, a rather dull rebuilding by Paley and Austin around 1876 with a half timbered gable over the porch. This hardly does this historic spot justice, however, because the stout tower is 15th century but probably incorporating some Norman stonework. There may be a Roman altar to Mithras also set into the tower. In the churchyard stands

the Halton Cross – an imposing monument constructed like a jig-saw from several Saxon crosses. It stands about 10 ft high and depicts Sigurd at his forge and surrounded by tools. There is also what seems to be a dragons heart roasting on a spit.There are some Christian figures still recognisable including scenes from the Crucifixion, as well as two dragons and a galloping horse.

On the opposite side of the church is the two tier family mausoleum of the Bradshaw family, the Georgian facade being constructed ready for the first to be buried there in 1760. In

Facing page:
Halton Cross near
the Crook of Lune,
one of the most
interesting
monuments in
Britain

springtime the churchyard is a mass of common flowers including dandelion, daisy and the delicate blue of germander speedwell. Looking out through the lychgate the imposing lump of Castle Hill – a pre-Norman motte – stands, its height and its atmosphere increased by the presence of a flagpole. Within the church there is a notice which reads "To those who might be tempted to secure unauthorised possession of our communion plate and to save the needless blowing of the safe the plate is stored in a bank by order of our insurers." What a sense of humour but also what a sad reflection of our times.

The White Lion pub is separated from the church by a stream lined with daffodils, Jack-by-the-hedge and yellow flag. Down in the village is the Old Hall (Tower House dated about 1760) which overlooks the Lune which is wide at this point and spanned by an iron bridge which is only about 5 feet wide and once carried a toll. Below it is a fine fishing spot, water flow improved by weirs constructed for mills which have long since outlived their usefulness. On the opposite bank is Halton station – now closed and shuttered – its platforms standing deserted above the footpath linking the Crook of Lune to Lancaster. There are splendid views from the footpath across the river to Halton church and motte. The footpath passes beneath the M6 and on the south eastern boundary of the parish is Rennie's famous aqueduct built in 1797 to carry the Lancaster Canal a staggering 50 feet over the Lune.

There are several things that the visitor to the area of the Crook of Lune can rely upon. A rich natural history, majestic scenery which has pleased poet and painter alike, flat walking and a spectrum of history from late Norman, through the middle ages, to Victorian England with canal, rail and road networks and then to a modern motorway which seemed to intrude when it was first built but has now settled so well into Lunesdale that it actually looks beautiful.

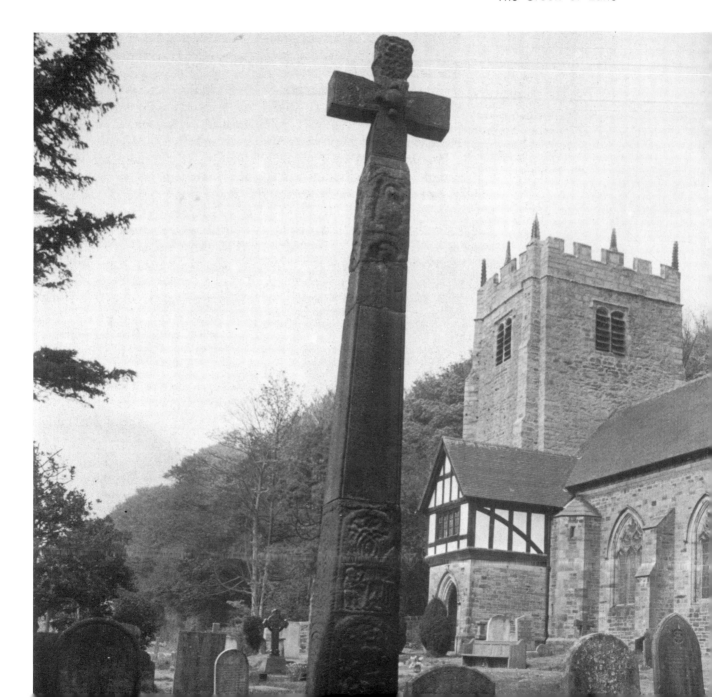

The Bradshaw mausoleum at Halton

Of all the old railway lines now converted into permanent walks amounting to linear nature reserves we rate this among the finest.

Stinkhorn fungus grows very well around the Crook of Lune in the wooded areas

Conder Green

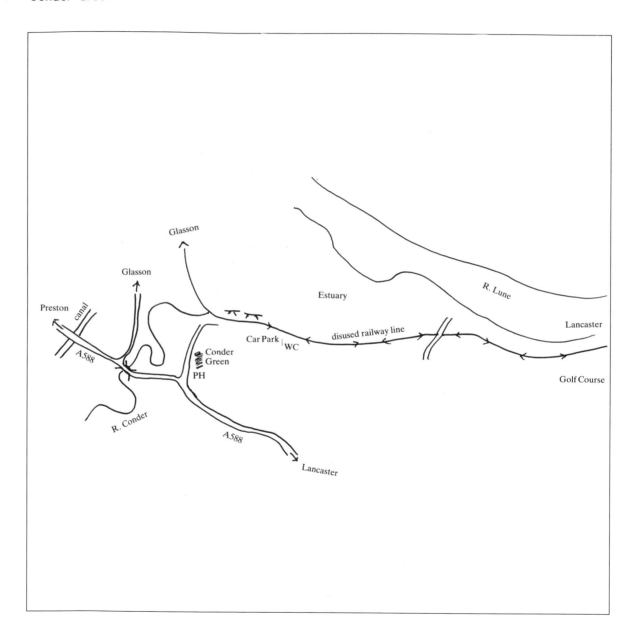

Walk Sixteen
Conder Green

ACCESS:

From the A588 road from Lancaster proceed past Lancaster Golf Club on the right. At the Stork Hotel turn sharp right and follow the signs for the Conder Green Picnic Site.

ROUTE:

Because this route is linear and flat strollers can decide how far they want to walk along the old railway track to Lancaster. Some prefer to go all the way to the Maritime Museum in Lancaster but is too far for most although it is easily reached in a day's gentle walking.

OUR WALK:

Glasson is a sheltered harbour on the estuary of the River Lune, described in walk no. 17, which is still used for commercial purposes, including the transport of coal, but the marina is a haven for seagoing pleasure craft heading out through the locks and out into the Irish Sea.

The surrounding salt marshes are equally popular with birdwatchers and botanists who seek out such plants as sea purslane, scurvy grass, sea aster, thrift, bittercress, orache, and whitlow grass, while spurrey, sea lavender and sea sandwort provide autumn colour as well as edible seeds for the birds. Most bird species, however, use the salt marsh as a roost emerging to feed on the mud flats. Ragwort grows well here and although it is poisonous to most animals including horses and cattle it is fed upon by the caterpillars of the Cinnabar Moth. These are

117

The cinnabar moth caterpillars feeding upon Ragwort along the old railway track around Conder Green

coloured yellow and black. Wasps are also yellow and black which biologists recognise as danger colours. Red and black animals also tend either to be poisonous or have a nasty sting. It seems that the cinnabar caterpillars eat the ragwort and concentrate its poison in their own tissues. It is interesting that adult cinnabar moths are coloured red and black.

From Glasson Dock a footpath follows the route of the old railway line which connected the dock to Lancaster via Conder Green, which has ample parking and toilet facilities, including provision for the disabled. Cyclists and horses also use the track, which is lined with a wide variety of native trees on which feed several species of butterfly and moth. In the summer their caterpillars are fed upon by whinchat, stonechat, dunnock and several other passerine species. The path continues to St George's

118

Quay at Lancaster, a distance of 4 miles. Along the length of the walk are a number of picnic tables and sheltered spots overlooking the area. Most walkers prefer not to walk to Lancaster, but to enjoy a short stroll up and down the track which is obviously flat and easy walking.

Before a final decision was made a number of schemes were discussed to run a line to Glasson Dock. In September 1845 the Preston and Wyre Railway Company put forward plans to connect Lancaster with Fleetwood and with a branch to Glasson. They did not have things their own way, however, and only a month later the York and Lancaster Railway proposed a line from Lancaster to Thornbush, which was close to Glasson, and there they wished to construct a new complex of docks. Neither of these schemes ever got off the drawing board and a railway did not actually begin operations until 1883. The line was constructed in three sections. These were Glasson Dock to Marsh, Marsh to St George's Quay and then on to Lancaster Castle Station. The only public station was at Glasson Dock although one was constructed later at Conder Green and there was a private stop near Ashton Hall – now Lancaster Golf Club's headquarters.

Rowan is one of the many trees growing along the track and its scarlet apple-like fruits attract fieldfares and redwings

After nationalisation in 1948 the authorities mentioned closure, but by 1969 the line ceased to function altogether after years of declining trade. Most of the track which was single line has been taken over by nature and is a fine footpath, surprisingly well drained and is a good walk in all seasons. "I love these railway walks" a friend once confided to us "you know you are not trespassing and there is no way you can get lost."

The view across the estuary reveals the village of Overton beyond which is a causeway leading to the one time cotton port of Sunderland Point.

Both sides of the estuary provide excellent birdwatching, especially in the cooler months of the year. Curlews fly into the Conder Green area to roost and we well remember a late November evening when the sun was sinking below the horizon. We watched over 800 curlews on the mud flats. In the surrounding fields 26 herons waited with great patience among a number of mole hills. These subterranean animals do spend more time on the surface than we often imagine and appear frequently in the diet of heron, short eared owl and buzzard. Lapwings, golden plover and an assorted group of gulls feed in the fields feeding mainly on the larvae of daddy-long-legs (cranefly). The grounds of Ashton Hall, now a golf club, overlook the path and the trees are ideal cover for pheasant, partridge and the occasional woodcock. Once the trees are loaded with ripe autumn fruits winter visitors such as fieldfare, redwing and blackbird enjoy the berries while long tailed tit, siskin and several species of finch take the dry fruits from the alder and willow.

At Glasson the marina provides an exciting combination of freshwater and marine ducks, with counts of up to 50 each of wigeon, mallard, teal, tufted, pochard, goldeneye, with the occasional red breasted merganser, scaup and eider. Wintering flocks of coot can on occasions reach 100 accompanied by up to 15 great crested grebe and moorhen. Oystercatchers do not reach

We found this "Thrushes Anvil" close to the shore near Conder Green. The clever song thrush collects snails and then breaks their shells by hammering them on a stone. Who dares call them "bird brains"

large numbers in this area of the Lune but several pairs breed along the shingle areas, while the salt marshes close to the area where the River Conder joins the Lune are breeding grounds for redshank, skylark and the occasional dunlin.

The coastal footpath walk can also be started at St George's Quay, Lancaster, where there is a maritime museum sited in the former customs house, which gives an idea of what life was like when the docks at Lancaster, Glasson and Sunderland Point were in full swing, fed by a railway which for one glorious period played a vital part in the prosperity of the area.

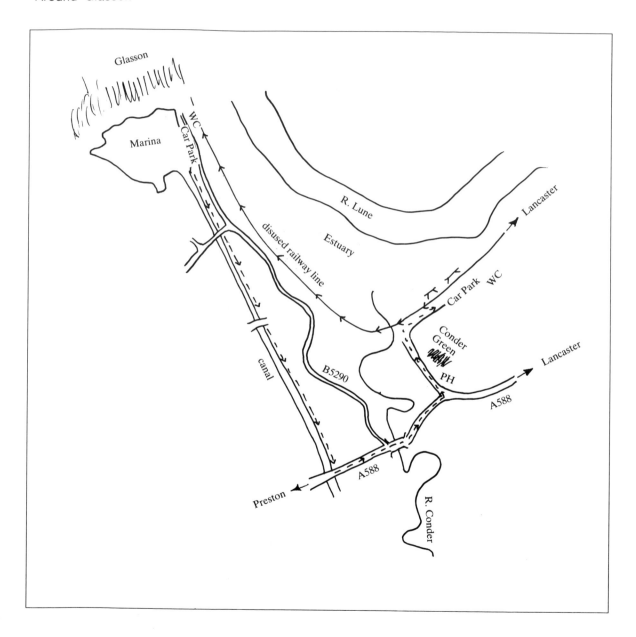

Walk Seventeen
Around Glasson

ACCESS:
From the A588 from Lancaster proceed towards Cockerham passing first the Lancaster Golf Club and then the Stork Hotel both on the right. Take the next turn right to Glasson. There is a large car park on the left for which a small fee is required. Glasson can also be reached from the A6 by following signs first for Cockerham and then to Glasson. There are toilets, hotels, restaurants and snack bars all close by.

ROUTE:
After exploring the dock proceed left from the car park and follow the line of the canal. Turn left onto the main road and return to the car park along the old railway track connecting Conder Green (see walk 16) with Glasson. There are excellent views over the estuary from this path. When the tide is in this is the place to watch for divers and ducks whilst at low water there are many waders here including godwit, redshank and ringed plover with goodly numbers of shelduck which also breed in the area.

OUR WALK:
There is so much to see at Glasson that it is hard to resist the temptation just to browse about, enjoy the cafes and pubs and not to walk at all! There seem to be boats everywhere – even a rather fine floating restaurant – and there are large vessels facing the sea and cabin cruisers facing the canal which was once an important link to the main line of the Lancaster to Kendal canal.

123

Glasson Dock is still busy even in the 1990s when many north-western ports have closed

In its day Glasson was well known for the building of sailing ships, but the main reason for its importance was as a dock closer to the sea than the port Lancaster, which was rather prone to silting up. When the first dock was built at Glasson in 1787 it could handle 25 merchantmen and soon took business from Lancaster and also from Sunderland Point. What a busy spot it must have been in the days of sail but unlike many north western ports such as Arnside, Silverdale, Milnthorpe and Greenodd, Glasson has not faded into history, but still works hard for its living with wood and coal being brought in from Eastern Europe.

We once made a film here for Granada Television and we were able to watch salmon being caught in a haaf net which has been in continuous use since the Scandinavians ruled this area of Britain. A haaf net looks like a set of soccer goal posts carried by the fishermen and held in the way of the moving tide, thus trapping fish by their gills. We also visited the small friendly factory producing smoked salmon. Each time we visit Glasson we take with us fresh bread and farm butter plus a bottle of white wine. All we need then is the smoked salmon to go with it. What a treat before setting out on our canal walk.

The canal seems to be a favourite haunt of swans and dragonflies. A couple of pairs of swans breed along this stretch of canal, whilst in the autumn and winter there are often several family groups competing for food offered by boaters and walkers enjoying a picnic. Any canal has many attractions for naturalists but this quiet stretch is particularly rewarding. As we enjoyed a picnic on a warm August evening we watched a pair of brown dragonflies hunting insects and swallows and swifts were also in evidence especially around the pretty little church snuggled close to the canal bank. Inside are many reminders of the days when Glasson Dock was working at full capacity.

The Dalton Arms, named after a prominent local family, serves excellent bar snacks

Dragonflies, including this brown aeshna, are a feature of a summertime walk along the Glasson canal

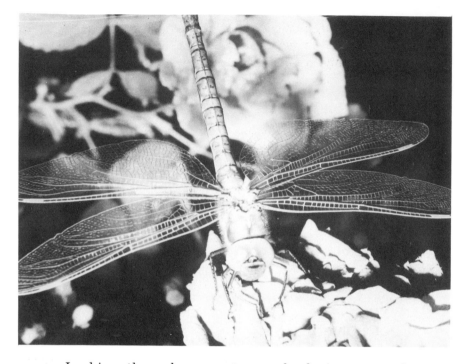

Looking through our notes made during more than 15 walks along this route we find that we have seen kingfishers three times, twice from the same bridge and on one day of gale force winds blasting in from the sea we watched 23 eiders and 11 common scaup, both species of duck which are usually more at home on the sea. Here they were content to shelter beneath the canal bridge and by the time we reached Glasson we were so tired after battling against the wind that we headed straight for the warmth of the Dalton Arms which serves good beer and provides excellent bar snacks at reasonable prices.

We were luckier whilst preparing this book and the day we chose to check our route dawned calm and clear with a warm April sun beaming down from a clear sky. A canal cruiser cut a white wake through the calm waters of the canal and the passage of the boat disturbed first a flock of coot, then a courting pair of mallard and finally separated a very aggressive cob swan from his pen who was busy attending to her nest among the reeds.

This is typical of Glasson, a gentle walk through history which is sure to provide interest whatever the weather or the season.

A family group of swans on the canal – a typical winter scene

Other books to look out for in this series –

NORTHERN CLASSIC REPRINTS

The Manchester Man

(Mrs. G. Linnaeus Banks)

Re-printed from an 1896 illustrated edition — undoubtedly the finest limp-bound edition ever. Fascinating reading, includes Peterloo. Over 400 pages, wonderfully illustrated.

ISBN 1 872226 16 7   £4.95

The Manchester Rebels

(W Harrison Ainsworth)

A heady mixture of fact and fiction combined in a compelling story of the Jacobean fight for the throne of England. Manchester's involvement and the formation of the Manchester Regiment. Authentic illustrations.

ISBN 1 872226 29 9   £4.95

Hobson's Choice (the Novel)

(Harold Brighouse)

The humorous and classic moving story of Salford's favourite tale. Well worth re-discovering this enjoyable story. Illustrated edition. Not been available since 1917, never before in paperback.

ISBN 1 872226 36 1   £4.95

NORTHERN CLASSIC REPRINTS

Poems & Songs Of Lancashire

(Edwin Waugh)

A wonderful quality reprint of a classic book by undoubtedly one of Lancashire's finest poets. First published 1859 faithfully reproduced. Easy and pleasant reading, a piece of history.

ISBN 1 872226 27 2   £4.95

The Dock Road

(J. Francis Hall RN)

A seafaring tale of old Liverpool. Set in the 1860s, with the American Civil War raging and the cotton famine gripping Lancashire. Period illustrations.

ISBN 1 872226 37 X   £4.95

The Lancashire Witches

(W. Harrison Ainsworth)

A beautifully illustrated edition of the most famous romance of the supernatural.

ISBN 1 872226 55 8   £4.95

The Best of Old Lancashire — Poetry & Verse

Published in 1866 as the very best of contemporary Lancashire writing, this book now offers a wonderful insight into the cream of Lancashire literature in the middle of the last century. Nearly 150 years later, edited and republished, the book now presents a unique opportunity to read again the masters of our past.

ISBN 1 872226 50 7   £4.95

THE STORIES
AND TALES SERIES

Stories and Tales Of Old Merseyside
(Frank Hird, edited Cliff Hayes)

Over 50 stories of Liverpool's characters and incidents PLUS a booklet from 1890 telling of the city's history, well illustrated.
ISBN 1 872226 20 5   £4.95

Stories & Tales Of Old Lancashire
(Frank Hird)

Over 70 fascinating tales told in a wonderful light-hearted fashion. Witches, seiges and superstitions, battles and characters all here.
ISBN 1 872226 21 3   £4.95

Stories and Tales Of Old Manchester
(Frank Hird, edited Cliff Hayes)

A ramble through Manchester's history, many lesser known stories brought to life, informative yet human book. Over 50 stories.
ISBN 1 872226 22 1   £4.95

Stories Of Great Lancastrians
(written Frank Hird)

The lives of 24 great men of the county, told in easy reading style. Complete with sketches and drawings, a good introduction to the famous of Lancashire and Manchester. John Byrom, Arkwright, Tim Bobbins, Duke of Bridgewater.
ISBN 1 872226 23 X   £4.95

More Stories Of Old Lancashire
(Frank Hird)

We present another 80 stories in the same easy, readable style, very enjoyable, great. With special section for Preston Guild 1992.
ISBN 1 872226 26 4   £4.95

LANCASHIRE 150
YEARS AGO

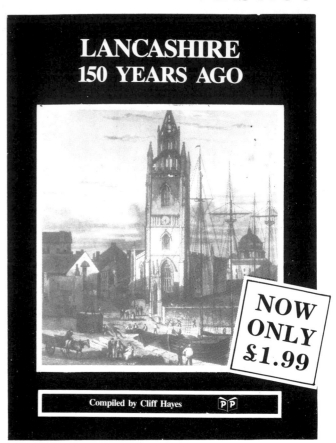

A great addition to the collection of any lover of Lancashire's history

OTHER BOOKS TO LOOK OUT FOR BY
PRINTWISE PUBLICATIONS LIMITED

MANCHESTER IN EARLY POSTCARDS
(Eric Krieger)
A pictorial reminiscence.
ISBN 1 872226 04 3   £2.50

CHESHIRE 150 YEARS AGO
(F. Graham)
Unique collection of 100 prints of Cheshire in early 1800.
ISBN 1 872226 07 8   £2.99

LANCASHIRE 150 YEARS AGO
Over 150 prints reflecting early
19th century Lancashire.
ISBN 1 872226 09 4   £1.99

BRIGHT AND BREEZY BLACKPOOL
(Catherine Rothwell)
Includes short history of the Tower and the Piers
ISBN 1 872226 13 2   £4.95

SOUTHPORT IN FOCUS
(Catherine Rothwell)
Glimpses of the town's past
ISBN 1 872226 15 9   £2.50

PORTS OF THE NORTH WEST
(Catherine Rothwell)
A pictorial study of the region's maritime heritage
ISBN 1 872226 17 5   £3.95

SUNRISE TO SUNSET
(life story of Mary Bertenshaw)
ISBN 1 872226 18 3   £4.95

THERE WAS A TIME
(Ken Loran)
Childhood Memories of Manchester and Salford
ISBN 1 872226 10 8   £7.95

OTHER LOCAL PUBLICATIONS

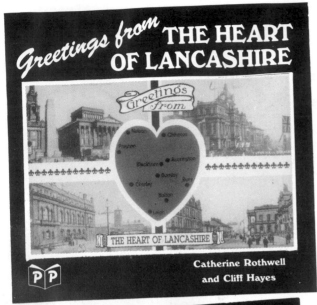

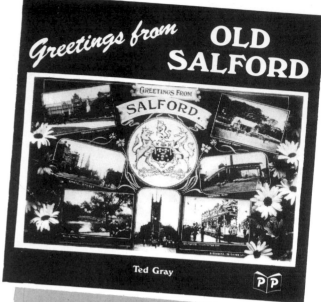

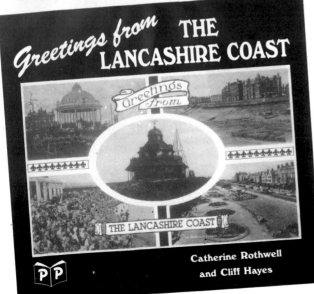

ALSO NORTH WALES; ECCLES;
AROUND MANCHESTER; LIVERPOOL